Green Infrastructure Finance: Framework Report

THE WORLD BANK
Washington, D.C.

Australian AID

ISBN (paper): 978-0-8213-9527-1
ISBN (electronic): 978-0-8213-9528-8
DOI: 10.1596/978-0-8213-9527-1

Library of Congress Cataloging-in-Publication Data
  Green infrastructure finance : framework report / Aldo Baietti ... [et al.].
     p. cm. -- (World Bank study)
  Includes bibliographical references.
     ISBN 978-0-8213-9527-1 (alk. paper) -- ISBN 978-0-8213-9528-8 (ebook)
  1. Infrastructure (Economics) 2. Sustainable development--Finance. I. Baietti, Aldo.
  HC79.C3.L3 2012
  332.67'22 -- dc23

                                                                        2012008110

Contents

Boxes

Tables

Figures

Foreword

In 2010 we published *Winds of Change*, a report that examined the carbon pathways followed by the rapidly developing countries of the East Asia and Pacific region (EAP), and what it would take to bend the carbon emission curve between now and 2030. The report concluded that embarking on a low-carbon pathway was feasible through stringent energy efficiency measures and innovations in renewable energy and other low-carbon technologies, but with a substantial price tag. The report estimated that in the EAP region alone about US$80 billion a year of additional investments would be required in low emission projects (green investments), resulting in a significant financing challenge.

The recent financial crisis affected a highly interconnected world, exacerbating the financing challenges overall and especially those for advancing the green growth agenda. Moreover, developing countries in the EAP region are witnessing major shifts in demographic and consumption patterns, with hundreds of millions of people moving to cities, investing in housing, personal transportation and various energy-using appliances. This places additional pressure on adopting best available technologies, building smarter cities, investing in low-emission mass transit systems, and in greening infrastructure.

The international community and national governments have compelling reasons to provide financial support to low-emission projects and to help them raise the needed financing, but public resources are limited. Moreover, the intrinsic characteristics of low-emission projects make them less financially attractive when compared against traditional but less eco-friendly alternatives. Elevated perceived risks and distortions in economies can further widen this financial viability gap.

The report argues that the solution lies in understanding the causes of the financial viability gap, and then investigating how specific actions, including strategic subsidies, concessional financing, and public policy interventions and reforms, can bridge this gap to make green investment transactions viable. More explicitly, the approach introduced in the report provides a framework for appropriately allocating risks and responsibilities, and demonstrates how to combine effectively multiple public and private instruments in a complementary fashion to maximize the leveraging effect of limited public sources of financing.

The green infrastructure finance framework also underscores the benefits of valuing and monetizing carbon externalities. Moreover, it recognizes the effects of policy distortions and other negative factors that impinge on financial viability, emphasizing the need for an approach to analyze and explain the gap and to attribute its components to different stakeholders. This report shows that it is essential to measure global and local externality benefits against the causes of the viability gap such as perceptions of added risks, cost differentials, policy distortions, and other factors. Once these elements are fully considered, policy makers can identify practical ways to better structure the financing of green investment projects that can be supported by the market.

The analytical framework lays out a simple and elegant way in which scarce global public financing can leverage market interest in "greening" infrastructure. It suggests mechanisms by which limited global public funds can leverage both national public funds as well as private financing in order to accelerate investments in low-emission technologies.

Three key principals have guided the development of the framework: (i) targeting green finance resources on sectors that have large numbers of projects with low abatement costs; (ii) setting ceilings on the value of support that will be provided for a tonne of greenhouse gas (GHG) abatement in any sector or project; and (iii) using competitive mechanisms to ensure that projects do not receive more support than needed to make them financially attractive. A fundamental prerequisite of this architecture is the establishment of a robust but easily understood and practical monitoring, reporting, and verification (MRV) system.

This report is the second of a continuing series of green infrastructure finance publications. The first part undertook a stocktaking of leading initiatives and literature related to the green infrastructure finance theme. This second part is a conceptual piece that bridges ideas and concepts between environmental economics and project finance practices. Work will continue over the next months by operationalizing this framework (analytical methodology and assessment of green infrastructure investment climate) through a pilot in a selected EAP developing country. Given a better understanding of the financing challenges of different green projects, work will also continue in developing more customized and innovative financing instruments that can be specifically tailored to address the requirements of these projects. It is hoped that the results of this work will help policy makers understand more clearly how to utilize global green infrastructure finance for scaling up investments in low-emission projects in their own countries.

John Roome
Director
Sustainable Development
East Asia and Pacific Region
The World Bank Group

Acknowledgments

This framework report has been prepared by East Asia and Pacific Region of the World Bank. The work was led by Aldo Baietti, Lead Infrastructure Specialist (EASIN) under the overall guidance of John Roome, Sector Director (EASSD) and Vijay Jagannathan, Sector Manager (EASIN). The team and co-authors included Andrey Shlyakhtenko and Roberto La Rocca (EASIN) from the World Bank, and David Ehrhardt, Alfonso Guzman, and Paul Burnaby from Castalia Advisors.

The team wishes to acknowledge those peer reviewers and other contributors inside and outside the World Bank Group including, Marianne Fay, Chief Economist (SDNVP), Veronique Bishop, Senior Financial Officer (CFPMI), Kirk Hamilton, Lead Environmental Economist (DECEE), Dejan Ostojic, Sector Leader, Sudipto Sarkar, Sector Leader, Alan Coulthart, Lead Municipal Engineer, Dhruva Sahai, Senior Financial Analyst, Migara Jayawardena, Senior Infrastructure Specialist, Xiaodong Wang, Senior Energy Specialist, Urvaksh Patel (EASIN), Magda Lovei, Sector Manager, Christophe Crepin, Sector Leader, Johannes Heister, Senior Environmental Specialist, Jaemin Song (EASER), Charles Feinstein, Sustainable Development Leader (EASNS), Richard Hosier, Senior Climate Change Specialist (ENVGC), Maria Vagliasindi, Lead Economist (SEGEN), Daniel Kammen (SEG), Ari Huhtala, Senior Environmental Specialist (ENV), Monali Ranade, Carbon Finance Specialist, Alexandre Kossoy, Senior Financial Specialist, Jose Andreu, Senior Carbon Finance Specialist (ENVCF), Russell Muir (CICIS), Moustafa Baher El-Hefnawy, Lead Transport Economist (ECSS5), Carter Brandon, Lead Environmental Specialist, Gailius J. Draugelis, Senior Energy Specialist (EASCS), Victor Dato, Infrastructure Specialist (EASPS), Rutu Dave, Climate Change Specialist (WBICC), Robert Do, President (Solena Group), Kumar Pratap (Consultant), 10EQS, Ltd, Salim Mazouz, Director (EcoPerspectives), and Tilak Doshi, Principal Fellow and Head, Energy Studies Institute (National University of Singapore). Edward Charles Warwick edited the report.

Finally, the team wishes to acknowledge the generous support from the Australian Agency for International Development (AusAID) provided through the World Bank East Asia and Pacific Infrastructure for Growth Trust Fund (EAAIG).

Acronyms and Abbreviations

AGF	High-Level Advisory Group for Climate Change Financing
BAU	Business as Usual
BRT	Bus Rapid Transit
CCS	Carbon Capture and Storage
CDM	Clean Development Mechanism
CEG	Clean Energy Group
CIF	Climate Investment Funds
CO_2	Carbon Dioxide
CTF	Clean Technology Fund
EAP	East Asia and Pacific
EE	Energy Efficiency
ESCAP	United Nations Economic and Social Commission for Asia and Pacific
ESCO	Energy Service Company
ETS	Emissions Trading Scheme
FiT	Feed-in Tariff
GCF	Green Climate Fund
GDP	Gross Domestic Product
GEEREF	Global Energy Efficiency and Renewable Energy Fund
GEF	Global Environment Facility
GHG	Greenhouse Gas
IBRD	International Bank for Reconstruction and Development
IDA	International Development Association
IEA	International Energy Agency
IFI	International Financial Institution
IIGCC	Institutional Investors Group on Climate Change
kWh	Kilowatt-hour
LE	Low-Emission
LSE	London School of Economics
MDB	Multilateral Development Bank
MRV	Monitoring, Reporting and Verification
MW	Megawatt
MWh	Megawatt-hour
NDRC	National Development and Reform Commission, China
NEF	Bloomberg New Energy Finance
OECD	Organisation for Economic Co-operation and Development
OPIC	Overseas Private Investment Corporation
PV	Photovoltaic
R&D	Research and Development
RE	Renewable Energy
RPS	Renewable Portfolio Standards
SCF	Strategic Climate Fund
SEFI	UNEP Sustainable Energy Finance Initiative

SPC	Special Purpose Company
TA	Technical Assistance
UN	United Nations
UNEP	United Nations Environment Programme
UNIDO	United Nations Industrial Development Organization

Executive Summary

The Financing Challenge of Green Infrastructure Investments

The International Energy Agency (IEA) estimates that to halve energy related carbon dioxide emissions by 2050, investments in energy supply and use should be increased by US$46 trillion over the business as usual (BAU) scenario. This requires additional investments of US$750 billion a year by 2030 and further investments exceeding US$1.6 trillion a year from 2030-2050. In particular, the energy portfolio mix should shift toward a significantly greater contribution by low-emission projects.

The *Winds of Change*, published by the East Asia and Pacific Region (EAP) of the World Bank in 2010, estimated that in the EAP region alone approximately US$80 billion a year of additional investments would be required in low-emission projects (green investments).

While the recent investment trends have been promising, the actual volume of investment is still well below desired targets. Bloomberg New Energy Finance (NEF) noted that investment in clean energy soared from US$34 billion in 2004 to approximately US$150 billion in 2007 and 2008—maintaining investor interest even during the global recession. However, while analysts differ in the exact figures, their conclusions are similar. Essentially, the current level of investments, and its anticipated growth, will not be sufficient to meet the challenge of global warming and the shortfalls are immense.

The question of financing green infrastructure investments, particularly *how* these investments are evaluated, designed, and financed, has still not received sufficient attention.

Status of Green Infrastructure Finance

To address this financing challenge, the EAP region of the World Bank conducted further work to assess the constraints in financing green infrastructure investments and to explore how investment opportunities could be improved in client countries. The first step of this work resulted in publishing *Green Infrastructure Finance: Leading Initiatives and Research*. This report not only summarized the status of activities in green infrastructure finance but also provided an analytical insight. A number of salient conclusions emerged from that study including:

- Public instruments and concessional funding are essential to leverage private flows.
- Green infrastructure finance requires country-specific public policies and instruments with the public sector taking the lead.
- Public and private sectors need to work together to develop unique solutions.
- In combining interventions some are more important than others.
- Many green investments are less financially attractive when compared against traditional but less eco-friendly alternatives.
- The financial and institutional interventions to accelerate green investments are numerous.
- Many green investments present unique risks because of their cash profiles.

▨   Distortions in economies can widen the financial viability gap of many green investments.

▨   While there are strong hopes that carbon markets can be revived, there is also great uncertainty.

The research report also concluded that a comprehensive "bottom-up" framework was necessary to assess the green investment climate in a given economy and to determine the appropriate mix of measures and instruments needed to best leverage limited public funds to accelerate private flows.

Benefits of a Green Infrastructure Finance Framework

The focus of this report is the green infrastructure finance framework. This framework bridges ideas and concepts between environmental economics and project finance practices. Three key principals have guided its development: (i) targeting green infrastructure finance resources toward sectors that have large numbers of projects with low abatement costs; (ii) setting ceilings on the value of support that will be provided for a tonne of greenhouse gas (GHG) abatement in any sector or project; and (iii) using competitive mechanisms to ensure that projects do not receive more support than needed to make them financially attractive. A fundamental prerequisite of this framework is the establishment of a robust but easily understood and practical monitoring, reporting, and verification (MRV) system.

The two-part framework consists of an analytical methodology for determining the financial viability gap and assessing and allocating risks associated with green investments as well as a comprehensive approach for assessing the green investment climate in a given country environment. By combining these two components, the framework aims to produce the following four benefits.

First, the evaluation and explanation of the viability gap can determine whether an investment can be justified on the grounds of climate change benefits through GHG emission abatement. It also explains how price distortions in an economy can have an impact on the viability of green investments.

Second, an analysis of the components of the viability gap suggests to policy makers how financing responsibilities can be shared between the national government, local government, and the international community.

Third, apportioning the viability gap among various stakeholders determines more accurately the mix of instruments that can be used to close the gap. This can combine international financing mechanisms with government instruments such as feed-in tariffs (FiT), direct subsidies, and fiscal incentives. The methodology also provides insight on how to use these instruments for maximum effect and at least cost to governments.

Fourth, the framework also helps identify actions that governments can take to improve various elements of their own investment climate, and thereby increase the scope for financing a greater number of investments to promote a low-emission economy.

The framework provides a basis for identifying green investments that can be financed and implemented within a current country policy framework as well as ongoing international programs. Such an approach helps identify investment projects that are not currently viable, but which can be made viable in the short term through blending financial instruments. In addition, non-viable projects that require substantive change in the investment environment can also be identified, along with the corresponding set of required policy interventions. Overall, the framework will allow policymakers to evaluate projects and develop a country-led green infrastructure finance plan.

Conceptual Methodology for Assessing and Allocating Risks

There are two main reasons why low-emission projects do not receive financing. First, the risk-reward profile of many low-emission projects is not financially attractive, either in absolute terms or in comparison to alternative investment choices. If these investment transactions were to occur, a financial viability gap would result or other investment choices would simply be more attractive.

Second, even in situations where green investments might be financially attractive, capital markets and information gaps may prevent private capital from flowing to these projects. For example, capital market gaps in low-emission projects are often the result of the "newness" of the technology or the process, and thus generate unfounded perceptions of excessive risk.

Factors preventing private financing flows are generally related to either high perceptions of risk, or high project or capital costs (for a given level of returns), or price distortions favoring fossil fuels, or a combination of all three. If it is the latter, then all three factors need to be analyzed so the risks are better allocated to the appropriate party and each party bears their equitable share of the financing challenge within a credible policy framework.

The outcomes of this analysis may vary for different types of low-emission projects. In general, low-emission projects can be separated into two categories: (i) capital intensive, infrastructure-like projects; and (ii) less capital intensive, corporate energy efficiency-type projects.

Capital intensive, low-emission projects occur predominantly in power generation or in major transportation infrastructure. These include renewable power generation, such as wind energy, solar, hydro, or geothermal power plants. They also include energy efficient transport infrastructure, such as bus rapid transit systems and rail projects. As with all major infrastructure investments, these capital intensive projects have large financing requirements and, like other major infrastructure investments, they are usually financed as standalone projects, utilizing "project finance" structures. In contrast, less capital intensive, energy efficiency-type projects have traditionally been financed on-balance sheet, and are financially distinct from the more capital intensive conventional infrastructure investments.

Capital intensive infrastructure projects have a number of distinctive features: (i) they require significant upfront capital and take many years to payback; (ii) output is typically sold on the basis of long-term contracts; (iii) and permitting risks can be significant. However, low-emission projects tend to have higher upfront costs; produce less output per unit of capacity; and have higher perceived risks than conventional infrastructure projects.

In summary, low-emission investments are more costly and have higher associated risks. For less capital intensive energy efficiency projects, the situation is different, and the extent of the barriers and finance challenges for various technologies differs markedly (as illustrated by the McKinsey GHG marginal abatement cost curve). Energy efficiency (EE) projects, such as street lighting, retrofit of buildings, and replacement of energy-using plants, machinery and equipment generate negative costs or positive returns and are typically considered financially viable with short payback periods. Yet, investment levels in these projects, particularly in replacement projects, could also be improved considerably.

Despite these challenges, low-emission projects generate more GHG emission and local pollution abatement benefits compared to a conventional infrastructure project and, therefore, create substantial public interest to monetize these benefits.

The international community and national governments have compelling reasons to provide financial support to low-emission projects and help them raise the needed financing. The international community has demonstrated significant interest in reducing global GHG emissions and has increased its role in funding investments on a concessional basis in order to reduce the effects of global warming. For example, the Clean Technology Fund (CTF), a US$4.3 billion trust fund with contributions from eight countries, was created specifically to support the development of low-emission projects. Other funds supported by the international community are also available or are in the process of being developed. Nonetheless, the amounts contemplated are still well below the required level of investment support.

National governments, while also interested in supporting global GHG emission reduction, recognize the specific benefits of low-emission projects, especially the ability of these projects to reduce other damages resulting from local air pollution and other local negative externalities. To realize these benefits and stimulate private investments in green infrastructure, governments could rebalance their own policy distortions with a mix of domestic instruments such as feed-in tariffs, direct subsidies, domestic carbon taxes, and other financing and fiscal incentives, thereby no longer disadvantaging low-emission investments.

In contrast, the international community could contribute international instruments for monetizing the global externality benefits of green investments through concessional financing and direct grants. Additionally, for projects that also propose to reduce local externalities, such as domestic pollution effects, governments could use an array of local and international financing instruments or even fiscal incentives to monetize those benefits.

The analytical framework lays out a simple way for appropriately allocating risks and responsibilities, and demonstrates how to combine effectively multiple public and private instruments in a complementary fashion to maximize the leveraging effect of limited public sources of financing. It suggests mechanisms by which limited global public funds can leverage both national public funds as well private financing in order to accelerate investments in low-emission technologies. Moreover, the approach not only identifies the financial structures that make investments viable, but also ensures that these structures are firmly grounded on economic principles and, therefore, that actions and contributions of each stakeholder do not create or amplify distortions in the economy.

In addition, green concessional finance could be used to monetize the value of net GHG emission benefits, while governments introduce other instruments to monetize the benefits of reduction of local negative externalities. The international community and governments should create a workable, if not necessarily optimal, combination of financing instruments that can attract private capital at least cost to the public.

This methodology guides policy makers toward better allocating risks and ultimately structuring the financing of these transactions while making use of multiple sources of funds. This requires the design of hybrid financing arrangements where parties bring in instruments for which they have a comparative advantage, and apply those to portions of the financing gap that are most appropriate.

Assessment of the Green Investment Climate in EAP Countries

Governments can play a pivotal role in promoting investments in climate-friendly technologies by adopting a wide range of interventions. Many EAP countries have proposed policies, programs, legislation, institutions, fiscal and financial interventions, and other measures designed to promote green growth of their economies through improving the investment climate.

A country's ability to alter the green investment climate and the effectiveness of their policy interventions differs according to the level of sophistication of a country's private financial markets, and the overall attractiveness of the country's investment climate. While in many cases the effort and the scale of public sector interventions is significant, the measures are often implemented in a piecemeal fashion without an overarching framework that includes a detailed assessment of the green investment climate.

The second part of this framework calls for an assessment of the green investment climate of a given country in order to develop country-specific recommendations. The overall evaluation of the investment climate of countries will provide general understanding of the attractiveness, prevailing trends, strengths, and other aspects affecting the ability of the country to alter the green investment climate. The framework is flexible and adaptive to the status and trends of the current investment climate of a given country.

The proposed assessment of a country's green investment climate consists of four main components: (i) policies and legislation; (ii) financial and economic instruments; (iii) programs and institutions; and (iv) regulatory environment.

Conclusions and Next Steps

The report presents a green infrastructure finance framework that can stimulate a greater flow of funds for green investments in EAP countries. It is primarily oriented toward promoting private investments, but can also accelerate public-private partnerships as well as purely public engagements.

The two components of the framework should be utilized together in order to identify green investments that can already be financed and implemented, given the country's current conditions and ongoing international programs. The approach can determine the investment projects that are not currently viable, but which can be made viable in the short term through blending financial instruments. Non-viable projects that require substantive change in the investment environment can also be identified, along with the corresponding set of required policy interventions. Overall, the framework will allow policy makers to evaluate the projects and develop a strategic green infrastructure finance plan.

Work will continue by operationalizing this framework in selected EAP developing countries. Given a better understanding of the financing challenges of different green projects, more customized and innovative financing instruments will be developed and specifically tailored to address the requirements of these projects.

More tradable permit schemes are being developed and emerging-country govern-ments should examine how to establish a cost efficient system of monitoring and verifi-cation in order to access the potential financial benefits and support that these schemes can offer.

Finally, developing a framework for improved collaboration between public and private sectors could greatly benefit green infrastructure financing mechanisms. This might occur through the development of a practitioners' network that would focus on knowledge exchange and on building working relationships.

CHAPTER 1

Rationale for Green Infrastructure Finance Framework

Introduction

The International Energy Agency (IEA) estimates that to halve energy related carbon dioxide emissions by 2050, investments in energy supply and use should be increased by US$46 trillion over the business as usual (BAU) scenario.[1] This translates into US$750 billion of additional investments a year by 2030 and over US$1.6 trillion of additional investments a year from 2030 to 2050. Additionally, the energy portfolio mix should shift toward a significantly greater contribution by climate friendly technologies. While such an investment trend has already begun, it is estimated that by 2020 investments will be at least US$150 billion a year short of the required levels.[2]

Recent World Bank and IEA studies have noted that a large proportion of this investment shortage will need to be provided by East Asia and Pacific (EAP) region countries. Thus, up to US$80 billion a year[3] of additional investments in low-emission projects and technologies (green investments) is needed to achieve these objectives, thereby "bending" the carbon emission curve (see Figure 1).

The Copenhagen Accord, followed by the Cancun Agreement, took significant steps toward mobilizing the necessary funding reaching an agreement to raise US$100 billion a year by 2020.[4] A High-Level Advisory Group on Climate Change Financing (AGF), established by the UN Secretary General, categorized the sources of funds into four groups: (i) public sources for grants and highly concessional loans, including the removal of fossil fuel subsidies, direct budgetary contributions and a variety of taxes on carbon and other transactions; (ii) the development of bank-type instruments; (iii) carbon finance; and (iv) private capital, as a major source of the total funding.[5]

The Advisory Group also indicated potential sources of financing that would allow scaling up investments in the developing world. In addition, the AGF emphasized the importance of maintaining a carbon price between US$20 to US$25 per tonne of CO_2, which would in turn generate an estimated US$100 billion to US$200 billion of gross private capital flows.

However, the question of financing green infrastructure investments,[A] particularly "how" green infrastructure investments are evaluated, designed, and financed has still not received due attention.

In order to address the financing challenge, the EAP region of the World Bank initiated work on assessing financing of green infrastructure investments and exploring how investment opportunities could be improved in client countries. The first step of this

Figure 1: Investments in Green Technologies and Emission Trajectory

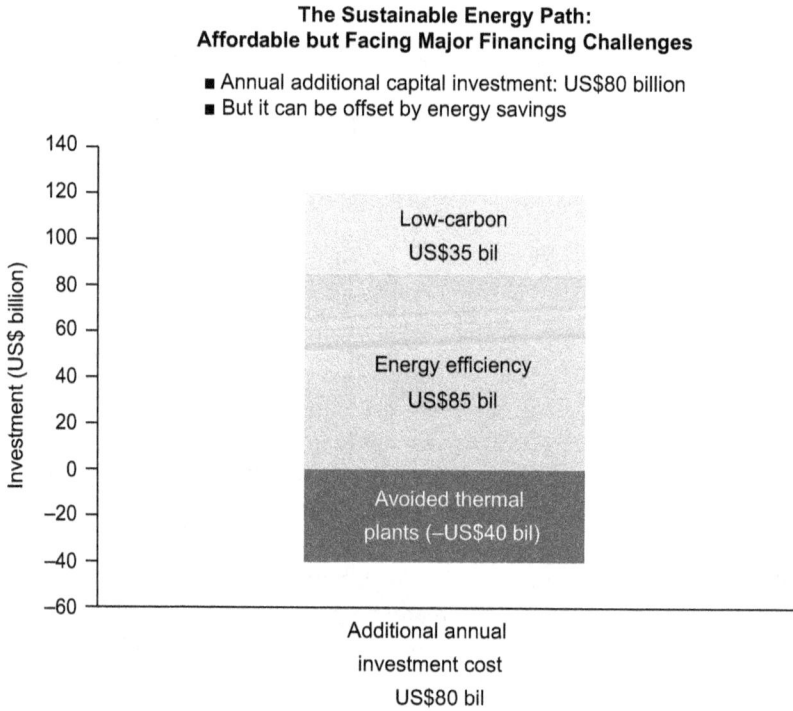

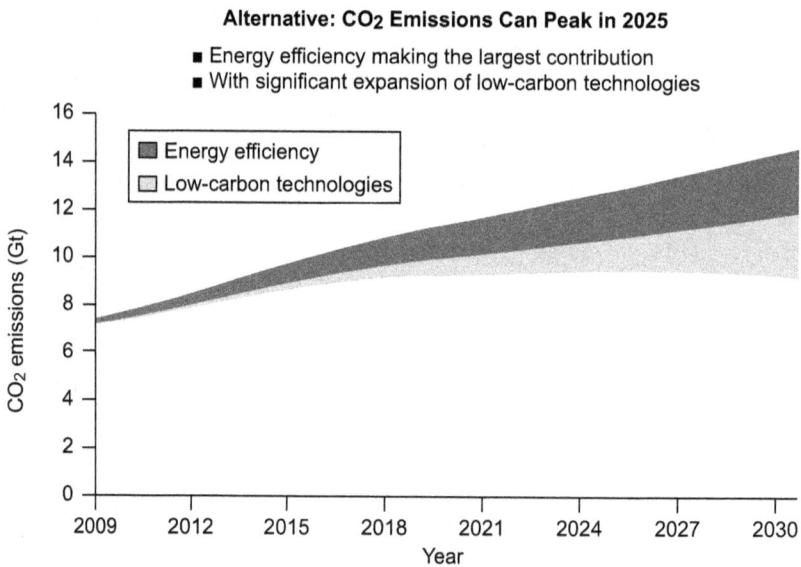

The Sustainable Energy Path:
Affordable but Facing Major Financing Challenges

- Annual additional capital investment: US$80 billion
- But it can be offset by energy savings

Low-carbon
US$35 bil

Energy efficiency
US$85 bil

Avoided thermal
plants (−US$40 bil)

Investment (US$ billion)

Additional annual
investment cost
US$80 bil

Alternative: CO_2 Emissions Can Peak in 2025

- Energy efficiency making the largest contribution
- With significant expansion of low-carbon technologies

Energy efficiency
Low-carbon technologies

CO_2 emissions (Gt)

Year

Source: Winds of Change, World Bank, 2010.[3]

work resulted in publishing *Green Infrastructure Finance: Leading Initiatives and Research*,[6] which not only summarized the status of activities in green infrastructure finance but also provided an analytical insight.

Main Conclusions from the Research Report

As previously indicated, green infrastructure investment demands are significant and the shortfalls in financing are immense. Essentially, "the current level of investments, and its anticipated growth, will not be sufficient to meet the challenge of global warming."[7] A solution can only be attained by a joint guided effort by public and private sectors, and a number of instruments should be combined for maximum effect. The research report further highlights the following key points:

Unfortunately, many green investments are less financially attractive when compared against traditional but less eco-friendly alternatives.

One of the principal barriers to attracting green investments is that many technologies and projects are not financially appealing, and as such, they will not attract investments purely by private finance without some level of support from the public sector. In addition, traditional GHG emitting investments, notably in the energy sector, are cost-effective to users, and therefore are supported by a financing and investment framework that is sophisticated, well organized, and well established. In contrast, the framework for financing green infrastructure investments is still in its infancy and its financiers have limited experience in scaling up to the required extent in this market.

The financial and institutional constraints to accelerating green investments are numerous.

Many studies[8,9,10] have focused on this specific point and show that low-emission investments differ from conventional energy projects "in five important areas: (i) transactions tend to be smaller, (ii) development activity tends to be led by non-traditional project developers, (iii) the availability and assessment of resources is very project-specific, (iv) projects tend to rely heavily on regulatory support and carbon pricing mechanisms, and (v) in some instances, projects rely on new or emerging technologies."[11] Further, green investments confront a range of additional challenges including information or knowledge gaps, confidence gaps, uncertainty over the protection of intellectual property rights, and political and regulatory risks. All of these challenges decrease the ability to reliably estimate the required rate of return and increase the associated risks and uncertainties.

Many green investments present unique risks because of their cash flow profiles.

Green infrastructure investments possess risks that conventional projects do not, or at least not to the same degree. These typically include demand and regulatory risks, risks associated with resource availability and quantifying benefits, and technology risks, among others. Moreover, green investments generally tend to be more upfront loaded with lower operating costs and, therefore, exhibit different cash flow streams than the traditional less eco-friendly technologies. For example, the initial upfront cost for energy efficiency replacement investment presents a greater burden in the initial financing decision, even though the project may be considered viable through a stream of offset savings in energy cost in the operational years. In addition, risk factors associated with different technologies need explicit consideration on a project-by-project basis. Such risks heavily influence the "hurdle" rate used by private sponsors to assess financial viability.

An elevated hurdle rate, in turn, further increases the disadvantages of the projects with greater upfront-loaded cash outlays.[12]

While there are strong hopes that the carbon markets can be revived, there is also great uncertainty.

Many proponents of green growth place great hope in a well-functioning carbon market with a predictably stable and appropriate global price for carbon. However, cap-and-trade regimes or tradable permit schemes have been difficult to operationalize because of political challenges in concluding a negotiations process. Nonetheless, developing countries that rely more on international assistance and which could potentially benefit from these schemes, should establish a credible and cost-effective system of verification, reporting and monitoring of GHGs.

The Clean Development Mechanism (CDM), Climate Investment Funds (CIF) and Global Environment Facility (GEF) have made major contributions to the financing of green investments and improvement of carbon markets. However, refinements are necessary to make these instruments more effective. For example, CTF's desire to maximize the leveraging of other financing depends substantially on the cash flow characteristics of individual projects as well the extent of the total externality costs inherent in a given green investment. As such, CTF funding of one investment can achieve a very different leverage ratio than another. Moreover, CTF might conceivably support projects already viable on their own, or alternatively, reward policy distortions in a given economy.

Distortions present in an economy can widen the financing viability gap of many green investments.

Policy distortions in an economy can favor traditional technologies. Several notable examples are subsidies for fossil fuels, and politically set tariffs that do not recover appropriate costs, as in the case of many infrastructure services (such as electricity, urban transport, water supply, and sanitation, among others). Depending on the magnitude of such subsidies, these may have a negative impact on the financial viability of a proposed green investment, or extend the required payback period beyond a level that investors and financiers are willing to accept.[B]

While most green investments confront similar financing constraints, the extent of such barriers facing different technologies differs markedly. As illustrated by the McKinsey & Co. study in its GHG marginal abatement curve cost, the finance challenges for green investments can vary widely between different approaches and technologies.[13] One set of investments—generally those involving improving energy efficiency initiatives—generates negative costs or positive returns, while another set, including renewable energy investments as well as the newest and unproven technologies such as carbon capture and storage (CCS), are fundamentally more costly, making them the least likely to attract financing from private financial markets. Currently, few instruments are available that can effectively shoulder "technology" risks in a cost effective manner.

Public instruments and concessional funding are essential to leverage private flows.

Most experts agree that concessional financing needs to be utilized strategically and that approximately 85 percent of the capital needed must come from private finance.[14] However, private financial markets behave rationally and require adequate returns after factoring in the various country, institutional, and project risks.

These "hurdle rates" are substantially higher in developing countries, especially if there are any perceived institutional and regulatory governance weaknesses. In addition, there are other more attractive investment opportunities (such as high-income real estate development) where the returns are higher compared to the perceived risks.

Under these circumstances, the private sector alone does not possess the incentives to mobilize financing to the scale necessary to lead this agenda. The private sector instead requires collaborative support from public finance as well as from international donors if the requisite magnitudes of financing are to flow into low-carbon investments.

Green infrastructure finance requires country-specific public policies and instruments with the public sector taking the lead.

The public sector needs to play a pivotal role in leveraging private financing because the "greening" of investments essentially requires mitigating externalities that are conventionally not valued by markets and investors. Public policies need to address issues related to carbon markets and taxes, regulations and standards, and financial support mechanisms as well as correcting policy distortions.[15] Currently, private investors consider that public funds (i) should be spent when commercial entities are not willing to invest; (ii) would be best utilized to make low-carbon technologies commercially viable; and (iii) should be used strategically at different stages of the technology development/diffusion process to leverage and attract private investments.[16]

In May 2010, the Organisation for Economic Co-operation and Development's (OECD) Council of Ministers interim report on green growth strategies articulated that both demand and supply sides must be addressed by policy interventions.[17] On the supply side, the interventions would include introduction of environmentally related taxes, tradable permits, charges, and fees, and the removal of environmentally harmful subsidies. On the demand side, the interventions would seek to influence the behavior of firms, households, or individuals through regulations and policies to support green technologies and innovation. In addition, voluntary approaches based on the dissemination of information and agreements between government, subnational entities, and specific industrial sectors should be considered. Other mechanisms and initiatives, including public education, are needed to stimulate more direct, rapid behavioral shifts among both the consuming public as well as producers with high energy needs.[18]

Public and private sectors need to work together to develop unique solutions.

The most recent collaborative approaches between the public and private sector have focused on specific issues or concerns rather than on developing broad arrangements for working together.[19] Private sector investors appear to be strongly motivated by the business opportunities available in green technologies provided—as long as the public sector demonstrates its steady and consistent support. In November 2010, the Institutional Investors Group on Climate Change (IIGCC), along with other organizations, jointly issued a simple but powerful message: "Investors are interested in the potentially large economic opportunities presented by a transition to a low-carbon economy. However, as governments lack strong, stable policies, investors do not yet see clean technology financing as viable."[20]

In combining interventions, some are more important than others.

Due to the distinct characteristics of green investments, some instruments and measures are more effective than others in closing the financial viability gap. For example, while the CDM provides benefit after the investment has been financed and is operational, a reduction of import duties lowers the initial capital requirements, yielding a more substantial return in terms of present value than another measure that amounts to the same nominal cost but instead enhances the revenue stream only in later years. Apart from the effects on the rates of return for a given investment, the reduction of the capital cost can actually facilitate the closing of the transaction financing as it reduces the initial sum of cash that would have to be raised.

The international donor community, together with multilateral development banks, has developed some innovative financial instruments and programs to offset the higher costs of viable clean technologies. However, more clarity is needed on how these financing mechanisms can be blended in a more effective and complementary fashion to address the inherent financing difficulties of green investments.

Governments still lack a comprehensive framework for assessing their investment climate for green investments and for determining an appropriate mix of measures required to accelerate capital flows.

A significant number of governments have proposed approaches in order to classify the broad array of possible public interventions. However, these attempts have not yet yielded a comprehensive framework tailored to country-specific environments to promote green investments.

Countries with well-developed capital markets are adopting pro-green policies at increasing rates and are also developing financing schemes and instruments for funding clean investments. Not only are they focusing on improving the global environment in addition to their own, but are also recognizing a major opportunity to develop and deploy as well as export their own green technologies to foster industrial growth along with its related income and employment benefits.

For less-developed nations, the options for national interventions are significantly fewer. Not only do these countries have limited capacity to compete in the field of technology, but their own public funding is constrained by budgetary restrictions and competing commitments from other important initiatives such as health, education and other basic services, including water supply and sanitation. Moreover, local capital markets and financial institutions of less developed economies still lack the capacity to create sophisticated instruments or mobilize long-term finance.

Consequently, many less-developed nations rely heavily on donor support through a number of international financing mechanisms. Nonetheless, governments could contribute to close the financing gap, especially in addressing policies that distort prices and disadvantage green investments in their own economies. It is therefore, essential that country governments are guided by a proper benchmark that sets realistic expectations for what can be accomplished in the short term and provides appropriate actions to make progress in both the medium and longer term.

The need for a structural approach in synchronizing and harmonizing the actions of all stakeholders is clear. Reliable methodology that can serve as basis of discussion is needed.

Green Infrastructure Finance Framework

In order to meet the need for such a framework, the EAP region of the World Bank has advanced its work on assessing the financing of green infrastructure investments and developed a *green infrastructure finance framework* aimed at delivering the following benefits:

- Explain and analyze the financial viability gap and, therefore, determine whether the investment can be supported based on emission abatement benefits. While any given investment may possess many facets and bring benefits along a number of different dimensions, the green infrastructure finance framework allows focus solely on the benefits generated through GHG emission reduction.
- Recognize explicitly the role of local and global externalities. The framework can provide insight into how to forge strategic support through policy reforms and international donor involvement in order to rebalance distortions, address local and global externalities, and attract private finance on the scale required.
- Through understanding of the components that comprise the financial viability gap, provide better guidance on which stakeholder is responsible for which portion of the gap. This may help initiate dialog between stakeholders capable of enacting measures to reduce corresponding parts of the gap.
- Identify green investments that are already viable as well as propose financial instruments that are required to make these investments a reality.
- For those investments that are not viable, formulate the spectrum of policy responses, including options that place a heavier (or lighter) burden on the international community, thereby alleviating the work for country governments or vice-versa. The framework may also provide insight into how to compare different integrated policy responses in order to choose an "optimal" one or the one with the highest funds mobilization impact.
- Tailor a balanced mix of solutions to a specific country context including those that can be implemented immediately (short-term solutions) and those that require policy dialog and building consensus (medium-term solutions). The former can be often achieved through blending existing and novel financial instruments while the latter require policy interventions aimed at altering specific aspects of green investment climate.
- Improve collaboration between public and private sectors through the development of a practitioners' network. Green infrastructure finance is a new area for policy analysis, and invariably involves a considerable amount of "learning by doing." In this context, this initiative is a welcome development along with those started by the World Business Council for Sustainable Development,[21] the C40 initiative,[22] the Carbon War Room,[23] and others.
- Help establish credible systems of validating that the green growth targets are actually being achieved. For this to occur, a cost-effective system of monitoring, verification, and independent disclosure is essential, to assure financiers that the GHG reduction outcomes are consistent with their targets.

Objectives and Scope of the Report

The objective of this report is to present a framework for accelerating financing of green infrastructure investments in EAP countries. The framework is divided into two main components:

1. An analytical methodology that provides an explanation of green investment opportunities in terms of market failure concepts and discusses how monetizing of local and global externalities can help close the financial viability gap.[C] It then proposes how a rational and efficient mix of policy and financing instruments could be developed in order to make these investments financially viable.

2. The second part of the framework focuses on what constitutes the key elements of a green investment climate in a given country environment. This makes it possible to identify investment opportunities, along with policy actions that can attract market interest in financing green investments.

This report focuses on mitigation investments in renewable energy (RE) and energy efficiency (EE), and is intended to benefit developing countries in the EAP region. This chapter presents an overview of the economic rationale[D] of green investments while chapter 2 lays out the foundation for developing a green infrastructure finance framework. Chapters 3 and 4 respectively discuss the components of the framework: financial viability gap analysis and country assessment. Chapter 5 concludes with a discussion on how these two elements can be integrated in a country context and lead to an action plan that promotes green infrastructure finance.

Audience

The results of this work are primarily intended to benefit governments throughout the EAP region and potentially will have spillover effects to other developing nations that are seeking to improve their approach for assessing and financing green investments. In addition, it is hoped that this work will also be useful to practitioners in this area, including existing fund managers seeking to acquire a better understanding of how to shape their criteria and operation guidelines for the utilization of their respective funds.

Notes

[A] Defined herein, "green infrastructure finance" is a combination of financial and nonfinancial interventions and instruments deployed by national governments and international donor community aimed at making low-emission investments in infrastructure more affordable and less risky to private sponsors and financial markets. The definition is applied broadly and beyond solely financial instruments on the conviction that financial interventions on their own can only deal with a limited set of solutions and complementary policies and programs are equally needed to make green infrastructure investments attractive. The term is used interchangeably with "green finance."

[B] Assessment methodologies not only need to consider what makes up the viability gap of many green projects, but also determine the respective roles of the various stakeholders including governments for closing it.

[C] The financial viability gap is defined here as a difference between net present value of project revenues and net present value of project costs. Net present values are calculated applying opportunity cost of capital commonly used by private investors for financing projects of similar nature.

[D] This report only focuses on certain aspects of economic benefits and does not account for others (such as health benefits). It is conceivable that some projects determined to be not "economically" viable and not justifiable may, in fact, be justified on other grounds not considered in this report.

CHAPTER 2

Economic Rationale of Green Investments

Climate Change: The Greatest Market Failure

The *Stern Review on the Economics of Climate Change* states: "Climate change presents a unique challenge for economics: it is the greatest example of market failure we have ever seen."[24]

Climatic changes, which can damage economies and livelihoods across the world, are caused by GHG emissions that are considered a "global negative externality" as the emitters do not pay for the costs they impose.

A GHG negative externality is, therefore, a "market failure" because market solutions are not socially optimal. For most products available in a well-functioning market, the market system works as a kind of cost-benefit calculator. The revenue received from the sale of the product reflects the economic benefits the products provided to consumers, while the costs reflect the economic value of the resources used. In this case, the profit criterion—that a firm will only make products where the revenue exceeds the costs—also performs a social cost-benefit function. However, when some of the costs are not included in the market mechanisms—as happens with negative externalities—the profit calculus of the market is no longer socially optimal.

Economic Policy Solutions for a Global Externality

There are standard economic tools for the prevention of negative externalities. These tools involve imposing monetary burden, for instance in form of pollution taxes, cap-and-trade systems, and, of course, regulation making it illegal to emit pollution above certain levels. However, these standard solutions rely on governments having the ability to impose regulations, taxes, or subsidies and the power to enforce them. These solutions become difficult to apply to a global externality, because there is no global government. Instead, such interventions require voluntary agreement between nations.

The Kyoto Protocol represented a step toward such coordinated action. However, not all countries signed the agreement, and the Protocol only imposes limits on some of those countries that did. The Kyoto Protocol is set to expire in 2012, but has not yet been replaced with any other global and binding agreement to limit emissions.

In the interim, the international community and national governments continue to work toward ways to cooperate in reducing GHG emissions. For example, the international community has committed to provide US$30 billion for the period 2010-2012 through a Green Climate Fund (GCF).[25] Another initiative, the Climate Investment Fund

(CIF), has current spending capacity of US$6.5 billion.[26] Such initiatives, collectively referred to as *green infrastructure finance*, are growing in importance. However, it is clear that this level of funding does not meet the level needed to finance required volume of low-emission investments. As discussed above, the estimated annual investment shortfall for climate mitigation and adaptation actions by 2020 will reach at least US$150 billion.[27] Only a fraction of the needed investments can be provided by actual commitments from the GCF and CIF.

As a result, the international community has recognized that the majority of new investment financing will need to come from private sources. Global financial markets can easily supply the volumes of finance required, but will only do so if the investments are attractive. However, many environmentally desirable investments do not offer a commercially attractive return.

Economic Principles for the Efficient Use of Green Infrastructure Finance

Green infrastructure finance resources are limited. Therefore, economic efficiency requires that green finance maximize its contribution to its intended objective of GHG emissions abatement. There are three key economic principles that, if followed, will tend to increase the efficiency with which green finance is used:

- **Economic principle 1**: Green infrastructure finance should reduce costs (or increase revenues) for low-emission investments, thereby offsetting the externality of GHG emissions, increasing returns on low-emission projects, and leading to more investments in low-emission projects.
- **Economic principle 2**: Funding should be concentrated on investments with the lowest cost per tonne abated.
- **Economic principle 3**: Financial support should not exceed the amount that is needed to cause investment in the project.

Economic Principle 1: Green Infrastructure Finance Offsets the GHG Externality

The lower costs, higher revenues, or lower risks offered by green finance offset the market failure that GHG emissions are not priced. This contributes to making conditions, which are currently tilted against low-emission projects, more equitable. Such a development will increase investment levels in low-emission projects.

One way public finance achieves this is by lowering the costs of projects, including reducing the costs of financing. By offering concessional terms—for example, below market interest rates, and longer tenors—green finance changes the returns available on projects. Other green finance mechanisms, such as CDM or feed-in tariffs, can increase the revenue investments earn.

Green finance is sometimes viewed as a means of providing additional capital. However, provision of capital is not the most important role for the public sector. Rather, the concessional terms that green finance offers can leverage private finance through changing the returns on projects.

Since concessionality is the attribute that makes green finance powerful, it is useful to be able to measure the value of the concessionality offered. By comparing the cash flows under a concessional finance option with the cash flows under a financing on market terms, the value of the concessionality can be derived. Any concessional financing can be considered as a blend of a grant and a loan on market terms (see Box 1). The grant

---

Box 1: Disaggregating a Concessional Loan into a Commercial Loan and Grant Components

---

Green finance is often provided in the form of concessional finance, such as CTF concessional loans. Concessional loans differ from commercial loans in a number of ways including lower interest rates, longer maturity periods, and payment grace periods. All of these factors are a form of concessionality—or subsidy—compared with commercial loan terms. Therefore, the value that concessional loans provide can be considered as a value of commercial loan plus a value of subsidy component.

The subsidy component can be calculated as follows:

$$Face\ Value\ of\ Commercial\ Loan - \sum_{t=1}^{n}[PV(i+p)_{concessional}]_t = Subsidy$$

Where:

PV = Present value (at commercial loan interest rate)

i = Interest payment

p = Principal payment

n = Number of payment periods

The subsidy component of the concessional loan provides the additional financial resource to a low-emission investment, and therefore recognizes the value of the GHG emissions reductions. However, the commercial component of the concessional loan can also be important where capital market imperfections can lead to a capital market gap—meaning that even commercial loans of desired tenor cannot be raised.

For the remainder of this section, references to the value of green finance for low-emission investments indicate the subsidy element provided by green finance.

Source: Authors.

---

component captures the value of the concessionality. This "grant equivalent" essentially makes the difference as to which investments attract private finance. The grant equivalent also represents the real cost to the public sector of the financing, and therefore is the scarce resource that must be used as efficiently as possible.

In the following analysis, references to allocating green finance resources are primarily references to allocating the concessionality. For simplicity, the analysis at this stage treats all green finance as though it were grants. The next chapter discusses the actual concessional finance structures that can be used.

Economic Principle 2: Projects with Lowest Cost per Tonne Abated Should Receive Priority

There will not be sufficient green finance to leverage private investments into all possible low-emission projects. Therefore, the scarce resource of public green financing must be used judiciously, to maximize the GHG abatement achieved. The guiding principle will be to target resources on those projects with the lowest abatement cost—the lowest cost incurred to abate GHG emissions by one tonne (see Box 2).

This is illustrated by a simple example. If building energy-efficiency projects need financial support of only US$5 per tonne of GHG abated, but solar photovoltaic generation needs subsidies of US$50 per tonne of GHG abated, then obviously US$50 dollars of green finance could abate ten tonnes if applied in building efficiency projects, and only one tonne if applied to solar photovoltaic generation.

In practice, the abatement costs of all projects cannot be known. Information costs prohibit any approach that requires all projects in an economy—or ultimately in the world—to be ranked from lowest abatement cost to highest and funded accordingly.

A similar result can be achieved in an information-economizing manner by setting ceilings for support. If a ceiling per tonne of GHG abated is set at a level that roughly equilibrates the demand for support from projects below the ceiling with the total value of support available, then the objective of concentrating scarce green finance resources on the projects with the lowest abatement costs will be achieved. The problem of setting the ceiling is nontrivial and is discussed further below, but this approach is clearly more analytically tractable than an approach requiring an actual ranking of all projects.

CAVEATS ON USE OF ABATEMENT COSTS

This report suggests that targeting green finance on the projects with the lowest abatement costs will be efficient. Given the importance of the abatement cost concept, it is worth clarifying some crucial points.

Box 2: Calculating the Cost of Carbon Abatement

The GHG abatement cost specifically examines the cost per tonne of abating carbon dioxide emissions for a low-emission investment.

The abatement cost can be calculated by comparing the net extra cost of a low-emission (LE) investment and dividing this by the amount of carbon saved.

$$Abatement\ Cost = \frac{(Cost\ of\ LE\ Investment - Cost\ of\ Current\ Energy\ Source)}{GHG\ Emissions\ Saved}$$

If a 2 MW solar photovoltaic farm costs US$7 million to build and has a useful life of 20 years, the cost of electricity generated by the solar farm can be calculated at **27 cents per kWh**. The solar farm displaces electricity generated by a coal-fired power plant, but the cost of electricity from the coal plant is only **7 cents per kWh.** However, the coal plant has GHG emissions of **1 kg per kWh,** of which the solar PV plant will abate. The abatement cost of GHG emissions by building the solar plant is therefore US$200 per metric tonne of carbon dioxide abated.

$$\$200/MTCO_2 = \frac{\$0.27/kWh - \$0.07/kWh}{1kgCO_2/kWh} \times \frac{1000kg}{metric\ tonne}$$

In this case, the abatement cost is positive, but abatement costs can also be negative. This happens when the project abates carbon while saving money at the same time. For example, consider a homeowner who pays a retail electricity tariff of **15 cents per kWh**, uses conventional 100-watt incandescent light bulbs, and wishes to install 40-watt energy efficient light bulbs throughout this house. The efficient bulbs cost US$5 each and last for eight years. Therefore, the cost of energy savings through installing the efficient bulbs is **1 cent per kWh**. Furthermore, the efficient bulbs displace coal-fired electricity, which has GHG emissions of **1 kg per kWh**. The abatement cost of the efficient light bulbs is US$140 per metric tonne of carbon dioxide abated:

$$-\$140/MTCO_2 = \frac{\$0.01/kWh - \$0.15/kWh}{1kgCO_2/kWh} \times \frac{1000kg}{metric\ tonne}$$

Source: Authors.

- **Economic versus financial abatement costs.** Most published estimates of abatement cost use economic cost concepts—they consider the real resource cost and benefits of projects, regardless of whether those economic costs and benefits are financial costs and revenues for an investor in the project. When leveraging private investments, however, only financial costs and revenues matter. As a result, this report references *financial abatement costs*, rather than simply *abatement costs*.

- **Static versus dynamic abatement levels.**[A] Traditional project evaluation tends to underestimate the dynamic effects of investments. In some cases, this can underestimate the levels of the GHG abatement that the investments will achieve. For example, evaluation of mass transit systems such as metros and bus rapid transit tends to assume that the urban form is constant. However, some transit system investments can alter the shape of a city. If the resulting urban form is more energy efficient, these dynamic effects can generate emissions abatement far beyond the static effects of traffic diversion to a new energy efficient mode. Similarly, some low-emission technologies—for example carbon capture and storage (CCS)—currently have very high abatement costs. However, if investments in early high-cost projects can rapidly drive costs down to competitive levels, then the dynamic benefits of future cost reductions should be considered when assessing the early projects.

Economic Principle 3: Only a Minimal Amount of the Financial Support Should Be Provided

Maximizing abatement for any given amount of concessional finance also requires that no project receives more support than the minimum amount needed to achieve financial viability and attract private investments.

This is illustrated by a simple example. If a building energy efficiency project needs a financial contribution of US$5 per tonne to proceed, but actually receives US$10 per tonne in financial support, some green finance resources has been wasted. It would have been preferable to pay the project only the US$5 per tonne needed to allow it to attract private capital to cover the investment cost. The remaining US$5 could then be used to support another project by leveraging more private finance and abating more emissions for the same amount of green finance.

Practical Principles for Green Infrastructure Finance Mechanisms

The above analysis shows that the economic objective for green finance should be to concentrate scarce concessional resources on projects with the lowest abatement costs, and to provide no more support to a project than is needed to make the project financially viable.

A strict application of this approach would suggest that all low-emission projects should be ranked from the lowest abatement costs to the highest. Green finance resources should then be provided to each project, exactly equal in value to the abatement costs, starting with the lowest abatement cost project. Progressively higher abatement cost projects would be funded, until the green finance resources were exhausted. If this method was used, total GHG abatement would be maximized for any given level of green finance available.

However, such a theoretically ideal approach is simply not possible. Policy makers cannot determine the exact abatement cost for all projects. Given limitations on information and government capacity, green finance programs need to be designed so that they can approximate the theoretical ideal, while recognizing that they cannot achieve it perfectly. Three useful tools can be applied: choosing sectors judiciously, setting ceilings for the value of support, and using competitive mechanisms where possible.

Focus Support on Sectors and Technologies That Have Many Projects with Low Abatement Costs

In any given country, some sectors will contain numerous projects with low emissions costs, while projects in other sectors will typically have higher emissions costs. Targeting green finance on the more promising sectors is likely to be the preferred option. Similarly, within any given sector, some technologies will tend to have low abatement costs, while others will typically have high abatement costs. Sound judgments about which technologies to support can therefore optimize the use of green finance

The sectors and technologies with the greatest promise will vary from country to country. In a country with abundant unexploited hydro or geothermal resources, the power sector may have strong potential for efficient abatement. Conversely, in a rapidly urbanizing country, the best options for efficient emissions reduction may be to ensure that new buildings are energy efficient, and to create efficient mass transit systems.

Set Ceilings for Support Provided per Tonne of GHG Abatement

In the theoretically optimal approach, green finance resources would be expended first on the lowest abatement cost projects, then on higher abatement cost projects, until resources were exhausted. All projects below a certain level of abatement cost would be supported, with no support for projects above that level.

The theoretically optimal result may be approximated by setting a ceiling on the grant equivalent value of concessional finance provided per tonne of GHG abatement. If the ceiling is about the level (in dollars per tonne) that would be reached under the theoretically optimal approach, then the final level of abatement achieved for any given level of resources will be close to optimal.

Setting such a ceiling can help ensure an optimal allocation of green finance resources between sectors, and across technologies. It would be inefficient to spend only US$10 per tonne on energy efficiency projects if solar photovoltaic projects were being supported with resources worth US$60 per tonne of abatement. Setting a ceiling would help optimize sectoral allocations. In this example, resources would be transferred from solar projects to energy efficiency projects until the abatement achieved from a dollar spent in each sector approximately equalized. In this way, the total amount of abatement would be increased.[B]

Similarly, within a sector, setting ceilings for support can help to maximize efficiency by improving the allocation of green finance across technologies and projects. In the renewable generation subsector of a particular country, for example, there may be many geothermal projects with an abatement cost below US$25 per tonne, while most solar projects have an abatement cost of US$60 per tonne or more. Setting a ceiling for support in such a case would help to direct resources to where they are best used—in this case, efficient geothermal projects.

This suggestion obviously raises the question of what level at which to set the ceiling. This is a matter for further analysis. However, it is worth noting that the UK government set a ceiling for internal government use in 2007 of £25 (US$40) per tonne of carbon emissions.[28] Another relevant value is the trading range of the EU-ETS. Also relevant is the UN High-Level Advisory Group on Climate Change Financing's recommendation of a carbon price between of US$20 to US$25 per tonne of CO_2.[29] (Solely for indicative purposes, this report assumes ceiling price of US$25 per tonne in subsequent chapters.)

Use Competitive Mechanisms to Avoid Excessive Support

Even within a given sector and technology, the actual abatement costs vary in ways that are difficult for policy makers to observe. Some energy efficiency projects will make a profit, while others need a subsidy before attracting private sector investments. One wind generation project might have an abatement cost of just US$20 per tonne, while another—in an area with a different wind pattern—might have an abatement cost of US$80 per tonne.

The problem for policy makers is that the actual abatement costs are often hard to verify. Private investors, although generally aware of their expected costs and revenues, and their abatement costs, may overstate their abatement costs, in order to increase profits by attracting additional financial support. From an economic perspective, this is a classic information revelation issue.

There is no perfect way to solve this problem. However, experience suggests two useful techniques. The first has already been mentioned—setting an appropriate ceiling on the level of support that will be offered. The second is to use competition. In a competitive setting, investors have an incentive to reveal their true abatement costs. For example, if a challenge fund for renewable energy generation was created, then all renewable projects would wish to maximize the funding they received. However, if the funding was allocated to those projects with the lowest abatement costs, then the temptation to overstate abatement costs is offset by the disincentive that this might result in the project not being awarded at all.

Achieving the right balance between setting ceiling prices and using competition will vary between sectors, technologies, and countries, depending on transaction costs and deal sizes. However, judicious use of these two approaches can result in green finance that is both practical and efficient.

Summary of Economic Design Principles for Green Infrastructure Finance

Effective green finance requires that limited public funds are used carefully to leverage private finance for low-emission projects. To achieve this, green finance needs to make a financial contribution to projects that reduce GHG emissions, thus making them sufficiently financially viable to attract private investments.

In principle, emissions reductions can be maximized if scarce public funds are concentrated on projects with the lowest abatement costs. In addition, no project should be provided with concessional funding beyond what is needed to make it financially viable.

In practice, it is not possible to identify precisely abatement costs for every low-emission investment. Effective program designs need to recognize this, and use other mechanisms to promote the efficient use of public funds. These mechanisms will generally include some combination of the following:

- ▣ Targeting green finance resources on sectors which have large numbers of projects with low abatement costs;
- ▣ Setting ceilings on the value of support that will be provided for a tonne of GHG abatement in any sector or project;
- ▣ Using competitive mechanisms to ensure that projects do not receive more support than needed to make them financially attractive.

The next chapter sets out how to calculate the level of green finance support needed by low-emission projects so that the principle of setting ceilings and limiting support to the minimum can be put into effect. It also outlines how to convert these economic principles into practical financial structures.

Notes

[A] An additional idea elaborated later in this report is the distinction between global and local abatement costs. Local abatement costs refer to the Sox, NO_x and suspended particulate matter that require financing from local or national governments. Abatement costs referred to in this report are only those related to reducing global GHGs.

[B] This rule can have greater leverage when local and global pollution abatement takes place jointly because technologies that reduce GHG abatement very often also "clean" the local environment.

CHAPTER 3

Conceptual Methodology for Assessing and Allocating Risks

Rationale for Methodology

There are two main reasons why low-emission projects do not receive financing. First, many low-emission projects are not financially attractive either in absolute terms or in comparison to alternative investment choices. This means there is either a "financial viability gap" so the project is not viable at all, or other investments are simply more attractive. Second, many green investments could be financially attractive, but because of other reasons, such as capital market gaps (or information or experience gaps), private capital does not flow to these projects. Capital market gaps in low-emission projects are often the result of the "newness" of the technology or the process, and thus excessive perceptions of risk. All these impediments need to be analyzed so that the risks are better allocated to the appropriate party and that each party bears their equitable share of the financing challenge within a credible policy framework.

Despite the challenges, however, low-emission projects generate more GHG emission and local pollution abatement benefits compared to a conventional infrastructure project and, therefore, may create substantial public policy interest to monetize these benefits. Thus, the international community and national governments have compelling reasons to provide financial support to low-emission projects and help them raise the needed financing.

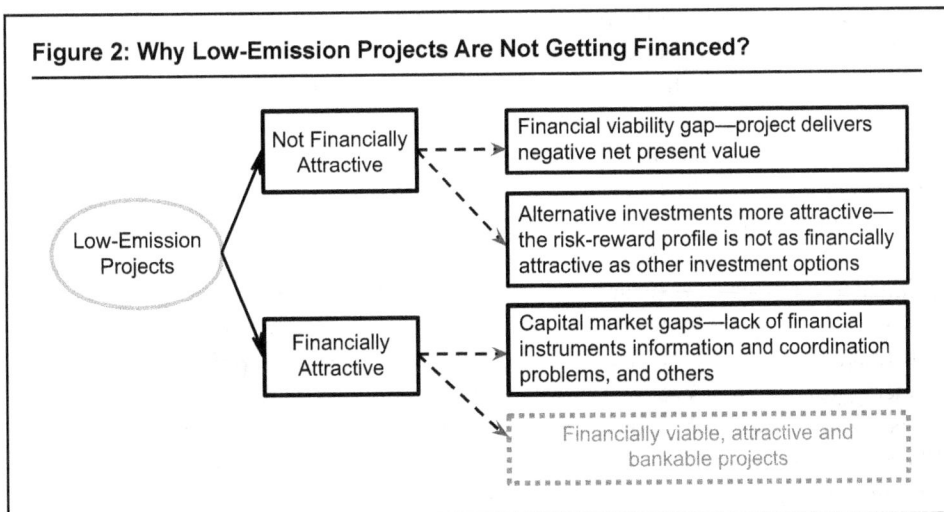

Figure 2: Why Low-Emission Projects Are Not Getting Financed?

Source: Authors.

The international community has demonstrated significant interest in reducing global GHG emissions and has increased its role in implementing international instruments for monetizing the global externality benefits of green investments through concessional financing and direct grants in order to reduce the effects of global warming. For example, the Clean Technology Fund (CTF), a US$4.3 billion trust fund with contributions from eight countries, was created specifically to support the development of low-emission projects. Other funds supported by the international community are also available or are in the process of being developed. Nonetheless, the amounts contemplated are still well below the required level of investment support.

National governments, while also interested in supporting global GHG emission reduction, recognize the specific local benefits of low-emission projects, especially the ability of these projects to reduce other damages resulting from local air pollution and other local negative externalities. To realize these benefits and stimulate private investments in green infrastructure, governments could rebalance their own policy distortions with a mix of domestic instruments such as feed-in tariffs, direct subsidies, domestic carbon taxes, and other financing and fiscal incentives, thereby no longer disadvantaging low-emission investments. Additionally, governments could use an array of international financing instruments incentives to monetize those benefits.

The approach presented under the Green Infrastructure Finance framework not only identifies the financial structures that make investments viable, but also ensures that these structures are firmly grounded on economic principles and, therefore, that actions and contributions of each stakeholder do not create or amplify distortions in the economy.

This approach provides a framework for appropriately allocating risks and responsibilities and effectively using multiple instruments and tools to make green investments viable. Further, these instruments could be applied in a complementary fashion and commensurately shared among the various parties. For example, in countries where the cost of coal is subsidized, governments could use feed-in tariffs to rebalance the financial impact of those policies thereby making low-emission investments no longer disadvantaged in that context. In addition, green concessional finance could be used to monetize the value of net GHG emission benefits and governments can introduce other instruments to monetize the benefits of reduction of local negative externalities.

The international community and governments need to create a workable, if not optimal, combination of financing instruments that can attract private capital at a least cost to the public. Therefore, the financing support structure adopted should address the specific reasons that prevent private investments, as well as help understanding specifically what each supporting stakeholder is paying for.

This chapter presents a methodology that addresses each of these steps, and in doing so guides policy makers towards better allocating risks and ultimately structuring the financing of these transactions while making use of multiple sources of funds. This requires the design of hybrid financing arrangements where multiple parties bring in instruments for which they have a comparative advantage and apply to portions of the financing gap that are most appropriate. As this approach is similar to a conventional project finance approach in infrastructure projects, understanding the similarities and differences between private investments in conventional and low-emission infrastructure should help better understand the methodology.

Similarities and Differences between Conventional Infrastructure and Low-Emission Investments

Low-emission projects can be separated into two categories: (i) capital intensive, infrastructure-like projects; and (ii) less capital intensive, corporate energy efficiency-type projects.

Capital intensive, low-emission projects occur predominantly in power generation or in major transportation infrastructure. These include renewable power generation, such as wind energy, solar, hydro or geothermal power plants; and energy efficient transport infrastructure, such as bus rapid transit systems and rail projects. Like all major infrastructure investments, these capital intensive projects have large financing requirements and like other major infrastructure investments they are usually financed as standalone projects, utilizing "project finance" structures (see Box 3). In contrast, less capital intensive, energy efficiency-type projects have traditionally been financed on-balance sheet, and are financially distinct from the more capital intensive, conventional infrastructure investments.

Capital Intensive, Low-Emission Investments

From a financing perspective, low-emission projects have much in common with conventional infrastructure projects:

- **Capital intensiveness requiring many years to recover the original investment.** Significant upfront capital is required for an asset base that will provide a service over the long-term, typically 20 years or more. To build the asset, both types of projects require long-term financing—often arranged on project finance, limited recourse basis where the majority of financing is typically raised as debt from a syndicate of banks (lenders). Under this financing arrangement, satisfying the requirements of the lenders, particularly for allocating risks, is a key consideration in deciding how the project will eventually be structured.

- **Output is typically sold under a long-term contract to an off-taker.** The special purpose company (SPC) created by the project sponsors will enter into long-term off-take contracts with a government agency or private company. This contract will set the terms under which the SPC will sell its output. These terms include output specifications, price adjustment formulas, as well as the payment terms. Under this type of contract, the SPC that owns the asset is exposed to the buyer breaching the terms of the agreement—for example, by delaying payments (payment risks) or not adjusting the prices according to the formulas set in the contract (regulatory risk).

- **Permitting risks can be significant.** Obtaining environmental permits can be more burdensome for high-emission infrastructure projects. However, both types of projects are exposed to a similar level of permitting risks as low-emission project confront similar permitting processes. Securing other investments or construction permits can be more onerous. For example, a wind farm has to acquire the rights to larger areas of land, dictated by the optimum location of the wind resource—this factor alone could make the permitting risk of wind farms more significant than for coal-fired plants.

Box 3: Characteristics of Project Finance

Most privately developed greenfield infrastructure projects are financed on a project finance basis. Investors and lenders prefer this financing structure because project cash flows and returns can be isolated from those of other investments. Clarity on project cash flows allows investors to identify risks that affect these cash flows and the return on investment, and adopt strategies for managing these risks. Project cash flows are commonly isolated from the balance sheet of a project sponsor by creating an SPC whose only purpose is to build, finance, and operate the project. The company will use contracts with specialized firms to transfer and manage specific project risks. For instance, engineering, procurement, and construction (EPC) services will often be outsourced to an EPC contractor, while operations and maintenance (O&M) responsibilities are outsourced to an O&M contractor. Figure 3 presents a simplified illustration of the structure that could be used to project finance a power plant.

Figure 3: Project Finance for a Power Plant

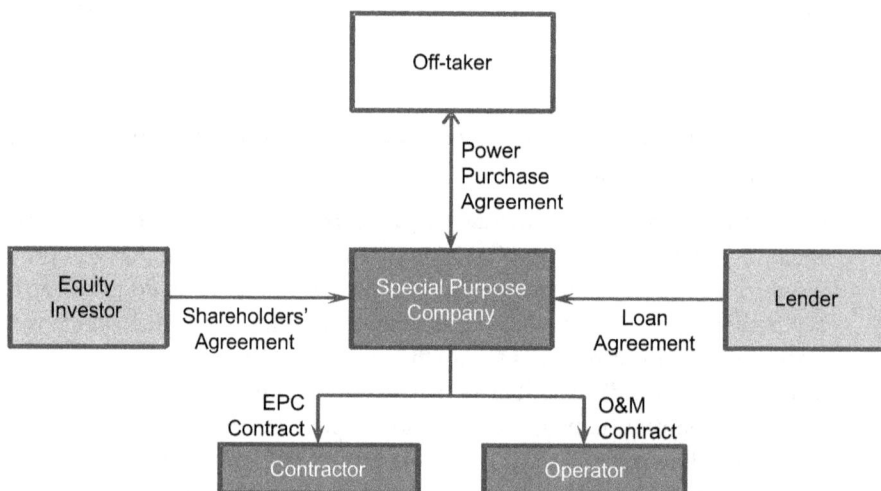

Source: Authors.

This structure gives equity investors and lenders a clearer understanding of the risks to which they are exposed, and the risk-adjusted return that they should expect from their investment. For example, by entering into a fixed-price EPC contract with a contractor, investors will transfer the risk of construction cost overruns to the EPC contractor, and could therefore reduce their return requirements—in relation to a structure in which the investors and lenders were directly exposed to this risk.

A key benefit of project finance is that it provides an effective structure to manage risks, and minimize the cost of risk and the overall cost of the project. However, this benefit comes at a cost. Creating an SPC and structuring and procuring contracts with specialized firms have significant transaction costs that are not scaled down if the size of the project is small. This means that smaller projects, with a capital investment of less than US$10 million, could find that project finance is not cost-benefit justified.

Source: Authors.

Many of aforementioned features, however, are more pronounced in case of low-emission projects, making them less attractive than conventional ones. Moreover, distinct characteristics of low-emission projects negatively affect all three key factors of project viability (revenues, costs, and discount rate), making it even more difficult to attract investments. These characteristics include:

- **Capital costs are higher**: Low-emission projects have higher upfront capital costs, and higher lifecycle costs than their high-emission alternatives. This means that low-emission projects: (i) need to raise more upfront finance per unit of capacity; (ii) need to pay more interest during construction, which further increases upfront capital requirements; (iii) pay more interest overall; (iv) require larger debt service reserve accounts as debt payments are higher; (v) incur higher upfront and commitment fees; and (vi) produce output at a higher price than high-emission alternatives—making it less competitive.
- **Revenues are lower:** Low-emission projects produce less output per unit of capacity than high-emission alternatives. The output of low-emission projects—for example, wind farms or solar plants—depends on natural sources of energy that are largely unpredictable. This means that the actual output of low-emission projects per unit of capacity installed is less than their conventional alternatives. Moreover, unpredictable variations in cash flow means that debt service coverage ratio may not be met as easily, making debt harder to raise, or requiring a lower debt to equity ratio—which could increase the cost of capital of the project.
- **Demanded returns are higher:** Low-emission projects have higher perceived risks than conventional infrastructure projects. The perceived risks can lead investors to demand higher returns, or can even become a complete barrier to investment when the risks exceed the levels that investors are willing to accept. Risk perceptions for low-emission projects are higher because the technologies used are often new to many countries, and there is limited experience in the country in investing, using, and maintaining these technologies.

These cost, revenue, and return characteristics are intrinsic properties of the low-emission projects and while technology development and penetration can positively affect them in the long-term, in the short-term they should be considered static. Often, however, an investment profile of the low-emission project is further disadvantaged by the actions taken by government that favor tradition projects and disincentivize low-emission investments:

- **Policy and price distortions:** Low-emission projects can often be disadvantaged compared with conventional alternatives by fuel subsidies and other price distortions. Such distortions include subsidies, tax incentives, and trade restrictions. For example, coal power is subsidized in Vietnam due to coal export restrictions that are placed on coal produced domestically. This, in turn, lowers the price of coal, reducing the fuel cost for coal power plant operators. These distortions often result in decreasing the revenue flows and increasing cost outlays for low-emission projects.

Examples of additional risks of low-emission investments are shown in Table 1.

Table 1: Additional Risks of Low-Emission Investments

Risks that are higher	Risks that are the same, but cost low-emission projects more	Risks that are perceived to be high, but may not be
• Resource availability • Non-traditional project developers lack track records • New or emerging technologies • Inexperienced local contractors • Non-investment grade off-takers • Regulatory risk from regulatory or fiscal support instruments	• Transactions tend to be smaller • Existing assets that are replaced may still have residual value that is greater than their salvage value	• There is a limited secondary market • Market unfamiliarity with investment class creates an irrational risk aversion

Source: Authors.

While low-emission projects possess these additional challenges, they also generate GHG emission and local pollution abatement benefits when compared to a conventional infrastructure projects. As a result, low-emission projects can create substantial interest to monetize these benefits, and use the generated revenue to offset some of the factors that make low-emission projects more difficult to finance. For example, the international community could "pay" the SPC for every tonne of GHG abated. This payment can be in many forms of financial support that have an implicit subsidy, such as an upfront grant or concessional loans or feed-in tariffs.

Table 2 illustrates the similarities and differences using a hypothetical coal-fired power plant and a wind farm. The shaded cells indicate the differences between projects.

Table 2: Technical and Financial Factors for Coal and Wind Energy Investments

	Coal-fired Power Plant	Wind Farm Power Plant
Technical and Financial Factors		
Capacity	100 MW	100 MW
Capital Cost	US$130 million	US$160 million
Off-take Contract	20 year PPA	20 year PPA
Capacity Factor	95%	35%
Cost of Fuel	Coal—US$60/tonne	Wind—zero
Financing	Project Finance: 70% Debt, 30% Equity	Project Finance: 70% Debt, 30% Equity
Key risks and their importance		
Permitting (environmental)	High	Medium/High
Construction	Medium/High	High
Variability of Output	Low	High
Uncertainty in Sources and Prices of Fuel	High	Low
Operation & Maintenance	Medium	High
Price Regulation	High	High
Off-taker Payment	High	High

Source: Authors.

Less Capital Intensive, Corporate Energy Efficiency-Type Projects

While most green infrastructure investments confront similar constraints to financing, the extent of the barriers and finance challenges for different technologies differs markedly (as McKinsey & Co. illustrated in GHG marginal abatement cost curve). Energy efficiency (EE) projects, such as street lighting, retrofit of buildings, new investments and replacements of energy-using plants, and machinery and equipment generate negative costs or positive returns and are typically considered financially viable with short payback periods. Yet, investment levels in these projects, particularly in replacement projects, could be improved considerably.

First, the financial viability of EE investments is significantly affected by the number and extent of distortions in an economy that favor traditional technologies. Subsidies for fossil fuels or politically set tariffs that do not recover appropriate costs include, notably, urban transport as well as water supply and sanitation. Such distortions affect purchase decisions for both new and replacement investments.

Second, unlike the more capital intensive projects, EE projects are typically financed on the strength of the entity's balance sheet, whether it is a corporate entity, a municipal government, some other public enterprise or joint stock company. Hence, the attractiveness of the investment may only play a secondary role in terms of access to financing. The financing may be denied because of the entity's poor overall condition despite the cost savings generated by the proposed investments.

Third, specifically for replacement energy efficiency investments, the difference between the depreciated value and the salvage value of an existing asset that would be replaced must be fully incorporated in the evaluation analysis as a deduction from the cash flow benefits of the new investment. For example, all costs associated with salvaging an existing, less efficient generator would have to be deducted from the benefits of the new investment. This problem is accentuated, for example, in a street lighting case, which would typically require the replacement of all the lamps in given lighting section, regardless of whether the lamps have significant differences in their remaining useful lives.

Moreover, if proponents gain very little from tax incentives, such as accelerated depreciation, the incentives to replace existing assets, while they are still in operational condition, are significantly reduced. While the current stock of fixed assets in developing countries is arguably lower than in developed ones, pointing to a strategy of greening an economy through growth rather than EE replacements, EE replacements should nonetheless be an essential component of a government's green growth agenda.

Fourth, even if an EE investment, replacement or otherwise, produces a positive rate of return that exceeds the entity's hurdle rate, the sponsor may still decide against it for a number of reasons. For example, given that an entity typically has very well defined financing limits which guide it in formulating its investment plans, alternative investment options besides the EE project may be more attractive because of: (i) strategic or business considerations (for example, expanding markets and production rather than improving efficiency; (ii) other investment choices offering higher rates of return than the EE project against the entity's financing limits; or (iii) the calculation of the benefit stream of the entity's other investments may be more reliable than those of the EE project (for example, calculating the benefit stream of improving the efficiency in buildings versus an outright investment in equipment for expanding production: see Figure 4).

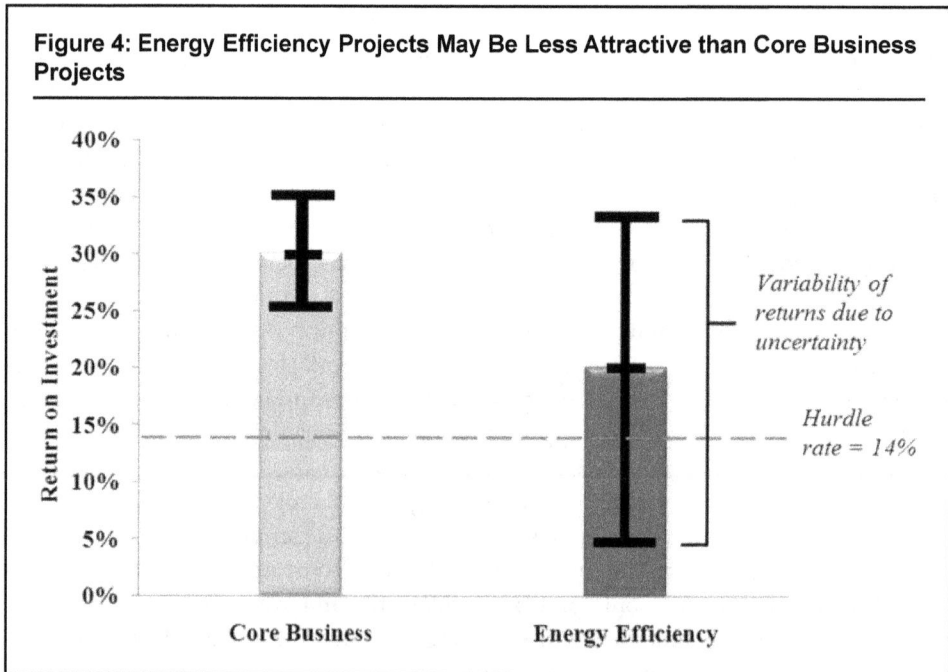

Figure 4: Energy Efficiency Projects May Be Less Attractive than Core Business Projects

Source: Authors.

Moreover, EE investments, like their more capital intensive counterparts, confront a series of other challenges such as capital market gaps, information or knowledge gaps, and confidence gaps.

Capital Market Gaps

Capital market imperfections or market failures are substantial obstacles in financing green infrastructure investments, particularly EE projects. In perfectly functioning capital markets, rational investors will deploy capital to all investments that are financially viable—investments that deliver returns consistent with their risk profile. There are three key reasons, however, why capital markets could fail to deploy capital to low-emission investments:

- **Lack of financial instruments**. Many of the EE and RE investments suffer from the unavailability of certain financial instruments. For example, EE projects often rely on ability of project sponsors to raise debt financing. However, lenders may not be willing to provide such loans as EE projects do not generate additional sources of revenue and, normally, do not offer collateralized assets. Similarly, RE projects require securing a long-term commercial debt with a tenor commensurate with the life of the project. However, this long-term debt financing instrument can simply not exist in emerging financial markets.
- **Information problems**. Energy efficiency investments are a good example of low-emission projects that suffer from information problems. Because the market for EE investments is nascent, project sponsors or financiers need to invest money and resources to perform adequate due diligence of opportunities—

thereby increasing the initial cost of sourcing information that eventually deters investor interest.

- **Coordination problems.** The nascent energy efficiency market in East Asia also suffers from coordination problems due to the lack of investors actively looking for, and investing in, projects, as well as the lack of project developers. When there are few buyers and sellers in a market it becomes difficult and costly to coordinate transactions because of a lack of market support structures that have been set up for efficient transactions.

Box 4 provides an example of the existence of a capital market gap in a low-emission project in Southeast Asia.

Box 4: Capital Market Gap for South East Asia Biomass Plant

A 17.5 MW power plant project, located in Southeast Asia, will use agricultural biomass to generate power. The plant will require a capital investment of US$61.2 million, which the sponsor plans to finance 70 percent with debt and 30 percent with equity. The sponsor has already secured debt from a local bank. Ninety percent of the debt is guaranteed by an export-import bank. The sponsor has also secured the electricity off-take agreements as well as the feedstock supply agreements.

The sponsor has been unable to attract private equity to close the financing of the plant. The question arises why investors have not been interested in this project. A capital market gap can partially provide an explanation.

The sponsor is a new company established by a group of industry experts yet does not have an operating history that is easily verifiable. As a result, equity investors would need to invest more time and money undertaking the due diligence of this investment than for other investments that could yield similar returns. This constitutes an information problem.

Further, this is the first biomass project in that country, and one of only a few in Southeast Asia. This represents a coordination problem, as there are very few participants in the biomass industry in the region. The equity investor has therefore limited options for sourcing the expertise needed to support its investment decision.

Source: Authors.

Understanding the Financial Viability Gap—A Wind Farm Case

The following example illustrates the problem of understanding the viability gap. Using the same wind farm and coal-fired plant parameters presented in Table 2, the wind farm project has a present value of revenues of US$60 million, and present value of lifecycle costs[A] of US$170 million—a viability gap of US$110 million. Figure 5 illustrates and explains the factors that constitute the financial viability gap for the project.

This financial viability gap for the Wind Farm case shown above can be explained by examining how low-emission projects differ from conventional projects. Besides higher upfront capital and lifecycle costs for low-emission projects compared to high-emission alternatives, the key differences include:

- **Low-emission projects have a lower output per unit of capacity compared with conventional generation projects.** This is caused by the intermittent characteristic of natural resources such as the wind and sun. For example, a produc-

Figure 5: Explaining the Financial Viability Gap for a Wind Farm

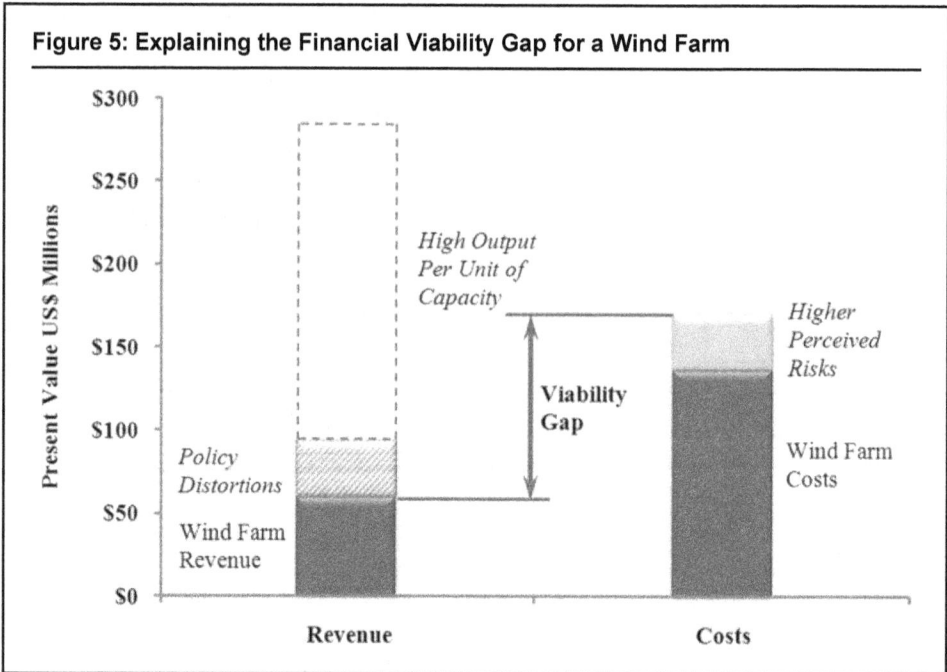

Source: Authors.

tive wind farm typically has a capacity factor of 35 percent, much lower than a typical coal power plant capacity factor of 95 percent. This has two implications that reduce the value of energy generated by a wind farm. First, because the wind farm is unable to operate as constantly as a coal power plant it will not generate as much energy revenues. Second, a wind farm needs to be supported by a reliable and dispatchable generation capacity that can provide power system stability when the wind drops. If a wind farm had a 95 percent capacity factor, it could earn US$200 million more in revenues over the project lifetime (see Figure 5, the tall bar on the left labeled "High Output Per Unit of Capacity").

- **Public policy distortions, such as subsidies, tax incentives, or trade restrictions, can disadvantage low-emission projects compared with conventional projects.** Such distortions can decrease the competitiveness of low-emission projects, partially neutralizing the key advantage of renewable energy sources—zero fuel cost.[B] In Figure 5, the impact of this policy distortion is depicted as foregone revenue (hatched portion on the bar on the left) caused by subsidized resources—in this example the foregone revenue has a present value of US$34 million.
- **Finally, the characteristics of low-emission projects lead investors to perceive them as riskier than conventional alternatives.** Coal fired power plants are well understood and financiers are better equipped to assess and manage their risks. Wind farms are new and still perceived as risky in much of East Asia. The apparent greater risk means that investors demand a higher return. If it is assumed that an investor expects a project-level return of 14 percent when investing in a wind farm, and 10 percent when investing in a coal power plant, the present value of the additional risk premium is US$33 million.[C] This cost is depicted as the lighter portion on the bar on the right of Figure 5.

As indicated above, the key reasons why low-emission projects do not attract capital include the existence of capital market gaps and financial viability gaps. To obtain financing for projects, one or both of these gaps need to be addressed. The goal of green finance can be viewed as addressing these gaps, and encouraging private capital by increasing the attractiveness of low-emission investments. How green finance can achieve this is explained in the next section.

Making Green Infrastructure Finance Work to Close the Viability Gap

Green finance can be used in two ways to close the capital market and financial viability gaps:

- First, by rebalancing policy distortions that cause some low-emission investments to be financially not viable;
- Second, by monetizing the benefits that low-emission investments create by reducing GHG emissions and local air pollution reduction.

Green finance helps to reduce and ultimately close the financial gap of low-emission projects by providing an economic rationale for the actions of each stakeholder and, therefore, minimizes the chances of creating inadvertent distortion.

Rebalancing Policy Distortions

As mentioned earlier, policy distortions that favor only conventional infrastructure projects can place low-emission projects at a financial disadvantage, leading to under-investment. Policy distortions, such as subsidies, tax incentives, and export restrictions, keep the price of conventional energy below its true economic cost. For example, in Indonesia retail electricity rates are highly subsidized—set at around 60 percent of the true cost of electricity generation. Likewise, in Vietnam, coal export restrictions reduce the cost of coal power generation by reducing the domestic price of coal. Such distortions are often harmful because they lead to increased energy use, the inefficient use of resources, and, consequently, to higher GHG emissions.

To encourage investments in low-emission projects there is a need to balance the policy distortions. The optimum solution would be to phase out such distortions, but this may be politically difficult. Instead, national governments could rebalance the distortions favoring conventional energy with a subsidy to low-emission projects. This would neutralize the distortions and ensure conventional and low-emission projects are treated more equally. If a government subsidizes energy consumption by 6 cents per kWh, it might choose to be consistent and also to subsidize, through various instruments, energy efficiency projects by 6 cents for each kWh saved.

Monetizing Reductions in GHG Emissions and Local Air Pollution

It is generally accepted that GHG emissions cause global harm. However, the harm is rarely accounted for in financial costs or revenues. For instance, in developing countries such emissions are often not subject to carbon taxes or cap-and-trade schemes that would attach a financial cost to the emissions. This creates an opportunity for financial instruments that in essence can pay low-emission projects for their GHG abatement, and therefore the benefit they create through emissions reduction. A well-known example of such an instrument is the CDM.

In addition to GHG emissions, there also exists the opportunity to monetize local negative externalities, such as local air pollution, that is reduced as a co-benefit of low-emission projects. For example, a coal power plant may emit harmful nitrous oxide and sulfur dioxide that cause acid rain and other environmental damage. A low-emission project such as a wind farm would not have such emissions, but its environmental benefits are not yet monetized.

Examples of Filling Viability Gaps

The following cases illustrate the opportunities for rebalancing policy distortions, monetizing GHG emissions, and monetizing local air pollution.

The 100 MW wind farm outlined previously has an estimated viability gap of US$110 million. This gap could be closed by rebalancing policy distortions, and monetizing the economic benefits from avoided GHG emissions and local air pollution (see Figure 6). The present value of the policy distortion is US$34 million. The economic benefits from the avoided cost of GHG emissions are US$102 million. In this case, financial support valued slightly higher than the GHG abatement benefits alone would be enough to close the wind farms viability gap of US$110 million.

Other non-monetized benefits can also be significant for some projects, such as urban transit. Figure 7 illustrates a Bus Rapid Transit (BRT) project for a second tier East Asian city with a viability gap of US$165 million. Monetizing the economic benefits of air pollution (US$35 million) and GHG emissions (US$25 million) does not close the viability gap. However, other non-monetized benefits that mitigate local externalities, such as reduced congestion, reduction in accidents, and productivity benefits total US$150 million in value. If certain portion of these benefits could be monetized through national or local government financing, the viability gap could be closed.

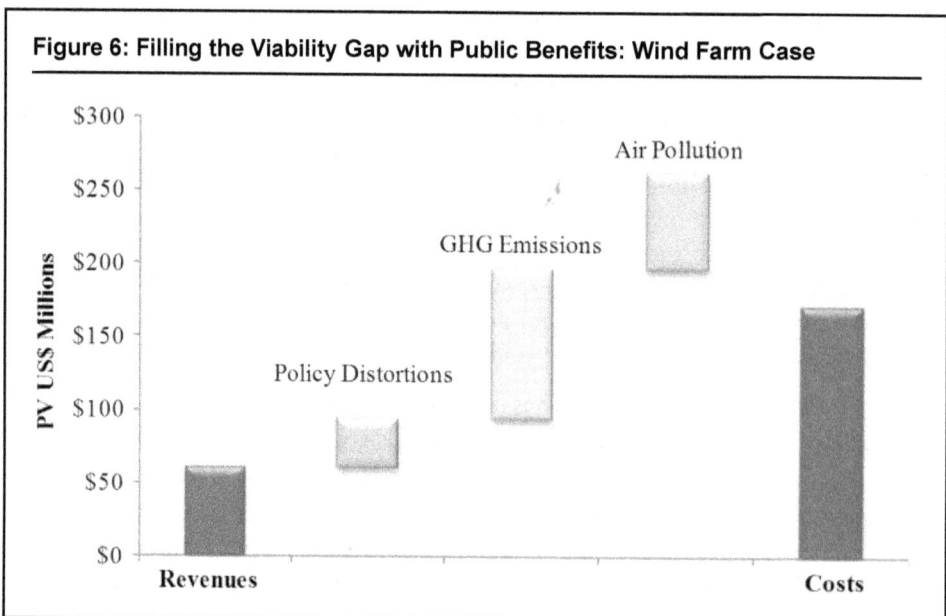

Figure 6: Filling the Viability Gap with Public Benefits: Wind Farm Case

Source: Authors.

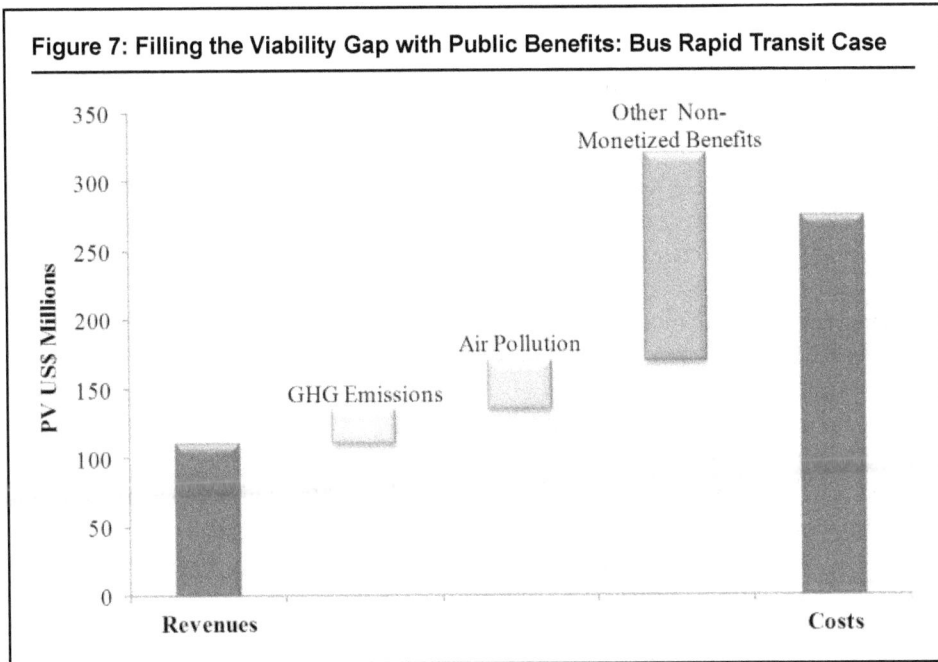

Figure 7: Filling the Viability Gap with Public Benefits: Bus Rapid Transit Case

Source: Authors.

Combining Instruments for Effective Financing Solution

The international community and national governments should find a practical combination of financing instruments that, with minimum use of public funds, would collectively close the gap and attract private capital. Therefore, the financing support structure adopted should address the specific reasons that are preventing private capital from flowing to low-emission investments, but do so at least cost to the international community or government.

This section addresses these issues by analyzing two important points. Firstly, by reviewing the role that the international community and governments (stakeholders) could have in supporting the financing of low-emission projects; and secondly, by describing the types of policies and instruments that these stakeholders can use to financially support low GHG emissions projects. Finally, examples of such projects show how these policies and instruments can be used in practice.

The Roles of Various Stakeholders

The literature and international consensus is clear—funding for low-emission investments must come largely from the private sector, but the international community and national governments should collaborate and demonstrate leadership to solve this challenge. The capital market gap and financial viability gap analysis above has shown that private sector finance will only be forthcoming if low-emission projects are made financially attractive or if the market gaps or imperfections that are preventing financially viable projects from being financed are resolved. A key role for national governments and the international community, therefore, is to use their financial resources and policy powers to help in closing these gaps.

A clear and appropriate allocation of responsibilities between the international community and national governments is important to ensure gaps are closed and private finance is attracted. Therefore, the international community should lead where payments for GHG emissions reductions are needed to close the gap, while national governments should lead on interventions related to national policy.

For projects that are not financially viable, monetizing GHG emissions reduction could close the viability gap, allowing private investors to deploy capital and achieve required returns. For other projects that are financially viable, but where the market has failed to invest, monetizing GHG emissions reductions could provide the necessary encouragement to private investors to deploy their capital. Given that GHG emissions are a global problem, the international community is well placed to contribute.

Low-emission projects will also benefit from rebalancing measures taken to offset the effects of policy distortions, and to reward them for reducing local air pollution. These measures contribute to closing the capital market and viability gaps, and can be justified solely with reference to the creation of local benefits. Therefore, there is a strong case for national governments to make the greatest contribution in these areas.

Contribution of the International Community

The international community has created a number of funding mechanisms for green investments. Specifically, the World Bank Group manages a wide range of windows that could be used to introduce tools and instruments that improve financial viability. Major windows include:

- **Climate Investment Funds (CIF)**—a US$6.4 billion facility that draws on the expertise of several MDBs to help developing countries pilot low-emission and climate-resilient development. CIF consists of two funds:
  - **Clean Technology Fund (CTF)**—aims to promote the demonstration, deployment, and transfer of low-carbon technologies through public and private sector investments. CTF provides support in the power sector, transport sector, and for energy efficiency projects;
  - **Strategic Climate Fund (SCF)**—targets three separate programs to channel financing for climate change mitigation and adaptation investments. The programs include the Forest Investment Program, the Pilot Program for Climate Resilience, and the Program for Scaling-Up Renewable Energy in Low Income Countries.

These funds are of course in addition to the non-climate specific windows of the World Bank Group including IBRD lending to middle-income countries, IDA concessional finance to low-income countries, IFC finance of private companies in developing countries, as well as guarantees offered by MIGA, the IFC and the World Bank Partial Risk and Partial Credit Guarantee products. Other notable climate finance modalities include:

- **Clean Development Mechanism (CDM)**—allows an Annex-I country with an emission-reduction commitment under the Kyoto Protocol to implement an emission-reduction project in developing countries. Such projects can earn saleable certified emission reduction credits, each equivalent to one tonne of CO_2, which can be counted towards meeting Kyoto targets. The CDM is the first global environmental investment and credit scheme of its kind.

▪ **Global Environment Facility (GEF)**—provides grants to developing countries and those with economies in transition for projects related to biodiversity, climate change, international waters, land degradation, the ozone layer, and organic pollutants. To date it has allocated US$9.2 billion, supplemented by more than US$40 billion in co-financing over 2,700 projects in more than 165 countries.[30]

▪ **Policy-oriented private equity fund-of-funds** such as the Global Energy Efficiency and Renewable Energy Fund (GEEREF)—GEEREF provides global risk capital through private equity investments for energy efficiency and renewable energy projects in developing countries.

In addition, individual country donors provide support through bilateral mechanisms such as direct grants and bilateral assistance. Some development agencies will provide grant assistance, some offer concessional loans, and technical assistance on sustainable energy policy. However, coordinating the wide variety of these different mechanisms in a complementary fashion and for maximum effect remains a challenge as many of these operate independently, applying their own operational guidelines.

Contribution of National Governments

Some national governments do provide funding to reduce GHG emissions. For example, the government of the Philippines is in the final stages of implementing feed-in tariffs for renewable energy.[31] This policy will increase energy costs in the Philippines, but will also help attract private financing to renewable energy projects, and so reduce GHG emissions.

In 2001, Thailand approved a feed-in tariff policy through their very small power producer program for renewable energy.[32] In 2010 alone, Thailand's renewable energy program unlocked US$700 million in low-emission investments.[33]

However, it is more common for national governments to provide subsidies that benefit conventional projects, inadvertently disadvantaging low-emission projects. For example, Vietnam's coal export restrictions disadvantage renewable energy projects. National governments should progressively unwind policies that provide disincentives for investors to deploy capital into low-emission investments but, while these policies persist, governments should provide equivalent financial support to low-emission projects to bring the investment conditions to parity.

Green Infrastructure Finance Policies and Instruments

A wide and diverse range of policies and instruments is available to the international community and governments to close the market and viability gaps that prevent low-emission projects from being financed by private investors. Most of them improve the viability of low-emission projects through targeting specific component of project viability (revenues, costs, and cost of capital). Table 3 lists some of the most important policies and instruments, along with the key advantages and disadvantages.

Table 3: Public Sector Policies and Instruments

Instrument	Advantages	Disadvantages
Revenue Policies and Instruments		
Clean Development Mechanism	• Pays directly for the desired result (GHG abatement) • Designed to pay up to the lesser of the viability gap and the value of the emissions reduction • Established scheme • Links directly to developed country carbon markets	• Difficult to coordinate with other financing Future uncertainty • Benefit is received after the project is already in operation and as such does not address the initial financing challenge • Costly for project sponsors to use • Relies on a burdensome regulatory framework for monitoring, reporting and verification
Feed-in Tariffs	• Typically tailored to the viability gap of particular technologies • Pays directly for renewable power • Highest price certainty to investors • Simple to administer	• Hard to calculate appropriate value; known to often pay more than the value of the GHG abated, or the viability gap, or both • Provides cash flow once the project is in operation; does not fully address the initial financing challenge • Tariffs need to be periodically reviewed and adjusted • Can be difficult to raise finance against
Renewable Portfolio Standards (RPS)	• Can help lower the total cost of that development • If enforced can meet RE targets • RPS imposes relatively low administrative burdens and direct administrative costs on those responsible for overseeing the policy	• The exact cost impacts of an RPS cannot be known with certainty in advance • Can be difficult to design and implement • An RPS is not necessarily suited to supporting diversity among renewable technologies, although an RPS can be designed to do so through the use of resource tiers and credit multipliers
Other Carbon Payment Schemes	• Pays directly for the desired result (GHG abatement) • Can be designed better than CDM in order to facilitate use in finance-raising, and lower costs	• Needs to be created • Unproven
Cost Policies and Instruments		
Capital Grants and Financial Incentives on Imports	• Simple • Can be targeted precisely to close viability gap • Quick in raising capital by forming part of the capital structure and reducing the amount of equity and debt financing required	• Because it is paid up front, there is a risk that the project does not ultimately deliver the desired results (although good design can greatly reduce this risk. The Government of India Viability Gap Fund for PPPs is a good example, particularly the way it integrated the grant funding into the senior debt disbursements).
Tax Credits and Other Tax Incentives	• Can offer a politically acceptable way to provide a subsidy in some countries	• The foregone tax revenue may have a real fiscal cost, but may not be accounted for in budgeting process, reducing the efficiency of public expenditure decisions • It may be hard to raise finance against tax credits and benefits only come downstream • Only pays out if a project is successful enough to generate revenues and/or profits. Many RE project do not generate accounting profits for many years in operation
Cost of Capital Policies and Instruments		
Concessional Loans	• Traditional approach • Helps provide finance directly at lower cost of capital	• Limited impact; may not fully cover the financing gap • Degree of concessionality is unclear, and so is difficult to target
Risk-Sharing Facilities	• Allows the entity offering the facility to directly target what it believes may be excessive risk perceptions	• Difficult to target to particular levels of GHG abatement • Unfamiliar, and so may appear complex and difficult to implement
Tax Equity Swaps	• Allows tax credits to be used more effectively by making them fungible between investors • Brings in equity contributions from companies seeking to benefit from tax offsets	• Creates complexity and risk for investors compared to more straightforward instruments such as capital grants • Like tax credits, may have real fiscal cost and, therefore, can distort public expenditure decisions
Direct Equity Investments by IFIs	• Provides risk-bearing capital. Equity is the cornerstone of the financial structure, and can mobilize other finance • Investment by IFIs can provide accreditation which attracts other investors and financing	• IFIs have relatively high transaction costs, meaning they can only do larger deals economically
Equity Investments through Private Equity Funds	• Creates highly incentivized investors • Delivery through fund managers can assist in project origination and knowledge transfer	• The most expensive form of capital. Demands high returns and has high transaction costs, and as such requires other forms of support to close the financial viability gap

Source: Authors.

Financing Structures

Green finance can enhance the viability of project-financed low-emission investments by targeting the characteristics that distinguish them from high-emission projects. Figure 8 illustrates (in the gray boxes) how some of the green finance instruments listed in Table 3 can be used to enhance project finance structure. This illustration represents a low-emission power generation investment—for example a wind farm—that will be financed using project finance.

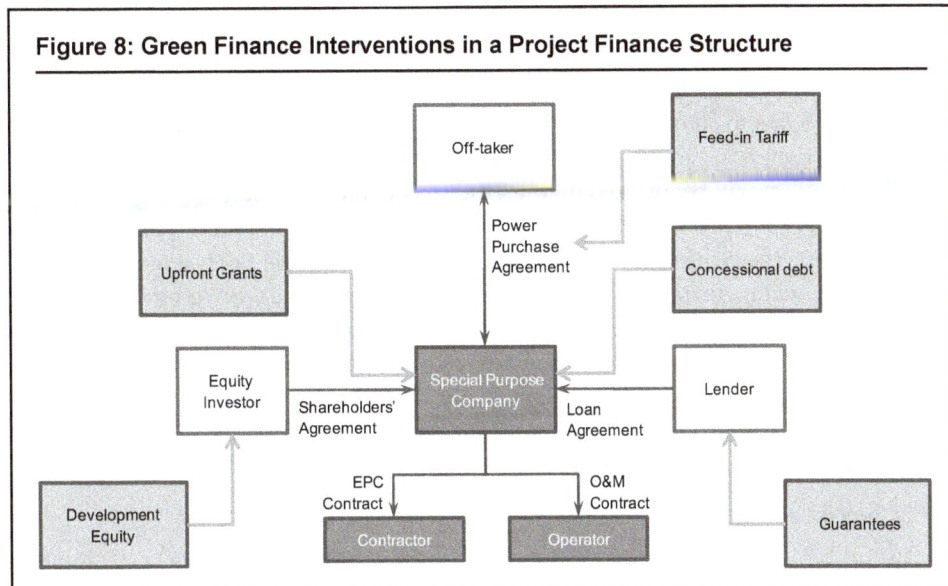

Figure 8: Green Finance Interventions in a Project Finance Structure

Source: Authors.

Some of the green finance interventions, designed to increase the financial attractiveness of renewable energy projects, could be applied as follows:

- **Feed-in tariffs (FiT)** or other public sector instruments could be used to rebalance policy distortions that disadvantage low-emission projects. For example, if the price of coal is subsidized through export restrictions, the FiT could be set at a level that offsets the subsidy on coal. The difference between the value of established FiT and value of short-run marginal cost of a coal-fired plant represents an explicit grant payment to renewable energy project. The present value of all these incremental payments reflects the total value of subsidy provided by the introduction of the FiT.

- **Upfront grants or concessional loans** that could be used to reduce the upfront capital investment or the cost of financing the investment if providing a FiT to rebalance the subsidy on coal is not sufficient to make the project financially viable. A concessional loan could be offered by one of the green finance facilities supported by the international community—for example the CTF. The concessional loan will have an implicit grant if compared to commercial sources of debt, as outlined in Box 1 in chapter 2. It would be economically justified for

CTF to provide a concessional loan that has an implicit grant value equal to or less than the value of the reduction in GHG.

- **Additional concessional loans.** If the combination of a FiT and implicit grant in the concessional loan is still not sufficient to make the project financially viable, it would be economically justified for the government to provide an additional concessional loan with an implicit grant equal to or less than the value of the local negative externalities avoided with the development of the project.

If the discussed interventions do not help achieve financial viability of the project or investors are still reluctant to deploy capital due to concerns about technology or resource availability risks, the international community could extend the support even further and provide a guarantee to cover some of these risks, or could provide equity or concessional loans to signal that this project is a sound investment. The guarantee and concessional debt have an implicit associated subsidy. The intervention of the international community will be justified on the grounds of emission abatement benefits if this implied subsidy is equal to or less than the value of the GHG emissions reduction.

If the joint application of all these policies or instruments fails to make the project financially viable then the project may need to be re-considered or other sources of monetizable benefits need to be determined to support the project fully. In some cases, interventions of international community may go beyond emission reduction benefits if there are other (preferably monetizable) benefits or if these particular interventions help achieve necessary economies of scale or create sufficient impetus for the technology so that the financial viability gap can become bridgeable.

Policy Support at Least Cost

It is useful to be aware of the array of policies and instruments available to the international community and national governments to support low-emission projects, and the maximum level of support that is economically justified for each. These policies and instruments, however, have a cost and a rational policy maker would certainly want to examine how these costs could be minimized and how these stakeholders can obtain the largest return on their investment. Furthermore, while the calculation of the financial viability gap is based on certain assumptions, the "actual" viability gap—the amount that investors will calculate as the gap—might be different. This leads to the question: How can the actual gap and the corresponding amount of financial support from stakeholders be set in practice?

One possible approach is to set the level of financial support through a competitive process. If the project is being tendered by the government, the project could be awarded to the sponsor that requires the least present value of government intervention. The intervention could be an explicit support, such as a subsidy or grant; or implicit, such as a concessional loan or guarantee. This approach would reveal the least amount of support that is needed to get the project privately financed.

This competitive process approach may not always be possible—for example, when the project is not being tendered by the government. Building energy-efficiency projects are a good example, as these are unlikely to be procured by the government. In this case, competition could be introduced at the stage in which the support (explicit or implicit) is being considered by the sponsor of the project. If there is an opportunity to compare two or more projects, the support could be given to the project that delivers the lowest abatement cost. However, if there is no opportunity to compare projects, the grant administrator could set a ceiling grant per unit of benefit (for example, dollars per tonne of CO_2 avoided) and award these grants to all projects that fall within that ceiling.

Examples on the types of green finance financial structures that could be used to support wind, geothermal, and energy efficiency projects are presented below.

Examples of Green Finance Financial Structures

Green Finance for a Wind Energy Project

The wind energy project, previously described in this chapter, is an ideal case to illustrate the complexity of the financing challenge for low-emission projects, as well as to underscore the reasons why certain instruments are more important than others—a conclusion of the stocktaking report. As was presented earlier, the 100 MW project has a cost of capital of 14 percent, resulting in a negative net present value, or a viability gap of US$110 million (see also Figure 9).

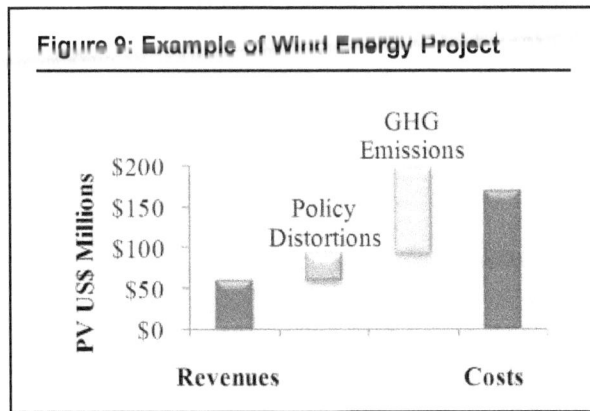

Figure 9: Example of Wind Energy Project

Source: Authors.

One reason why the project is not financially viable is because the price of coal is subsidized. In this case, the subsidy reduces the short run marginal cost of a coal-fired plant by 1.7 cents per kWh (from 4.7 cents to 3.0 cents per kWh), which in turn, reduces the avoided cost to the off-taker, and ultimately the price that the off-taker would pay to the sponsor of the wind farm. In order to rebalance this distortion, a government has a number of options including deploying the FiT instrument—the instrument that has already been introduced by many governments in the EAP region to support clean energy projects. In this case, the distortion can be corrected with a FiT of 4.7 cents per kWh—the rate that brings the price of electricity in-line with the avoided cost of a non-subsidized coal-fired plant. The rate also reduces the financial viability gap of the project by US$34 million.[D] Although widely utilized, this tool has often been adopted without considering the avoided cost of the energy displaced. Box 5 presents a good example in the Philippines.

Once the policy distortions are corrected, the remaining gap can be closed through instruments that monetize the benefits of the project's global externality benefits (which are estimated at US$102 million within this illustration) or local air pollution reduction (not shown in this example). In this case, a CTF concessional loan could be utilized in order to reduce the cost of capital, such that the US$76 million (US$110–US$34 million) remaining gap is closed.

Table 4 shows an example of possible financing structure through this arrangement. The FiT and the CTF loan are combined in order to close the financial viability gap of US$110 million, and thereby attract the investments. However, the CTF loan would carry a heavy burden in this structure, with a US$100 million or 62.5 percent contribution to

---

Box 5: Feed-in Tariffs

The feed-in tariff (FiT) is a premium rate paid for electricity fed back to the grid from a renewable energy generation plant. Many countries set FiT at a level that reflects the true cost of the renewable generation plant that is displacing conventional generation sources.

For example, the government of the Philippines has announced its intention to set FiTs. For wind farms, the government intends to set a FiT of 24.3 cents per kWh. This tariff reflects the government's estimate of the true cost of a privately financed wind farm in the Philippines. The true cost of a privately financed wind farm varies depending on the location of the farm, grid conditions, and other factors. In favorable cases it may be significantly lower, requiring lower FiT to bring the project to financial viability. However, in any circumstances this level is substantially higher than 4.7 cents per kWh—the avoided cost of a non-subsidized coal-fired plant.

Setting the FiT at such a high level may support a private finance structure, but also creates strong opposition—as has been the case in the Philippines—from consumer groups. This opposition—as it might be case in the Philippines—can block the adoption of these policies and therefore the development of privately financed renewable energy projects that are bankable.

Source: Authors.

Table 4: Financial Structure for Wind Energy Project—Needed CTF Support

Financial Instrument	Amount	Maturity	Grace Period	Cost of Capital	Subsidy
Feed-in Tariff	4.7 cents/kWh	—	—	—	US$34 million
Concessional Loan	US$100 million	20 years	5 years	0.9%	US$76 million
Sponsor's Equity	US$18 million	—	—	22%	—
Commercial Debt	US$42 million	20 years	—	11%	—
Total	US$160 million				US$110 million

Source: Authors.

the overall financing. While this financing is a possible solution, it is not a good leverage of limited public funds as it mobilizes only US$0.60 of private capital for every US$1 of CTF funds.

Moreover, this structure, while technically feasible, presents other challenges as CTF funding rules seek a high leveraging factor and is usually capped at around 25 percent of the total financing requirement, allowing for no more than US$40 million of CTF loan. This constraint leaves an unfunded viability gap of US$45 million. In most cases, this project would not proceed.

The above discussion illustrates the financing dilemma confronting these projects. Governments can set FiT tariffs that exceed the avoided costs, and face political criticism from consumers and other key stakeholders. However, increasing the amount of concessional financing is constrained by other factors. Notably, both are not optimum policy choices.

Another difficulty that arises from applying the FiT solution is that FiT payments do not help satisfy initial capital funding requirements. The FiT revenue provides its contribution over the operational phase of the project, instead of an upfront payment, when the capital is most needed. As many low-emission projects are significantly upfront loaded, raising upfront capital may at times become a substantial constraint.

To overcome this constraint, the subsidy component of the FiT (1.7 cents per kWh) could be securitized as an upfront grant. The funds provided by the securitization facility will get repaid over the life of PPA agreement by diverting the subsidy portion of the FiT revenue from the wind farm operator to the securitization facility.

Perhaps the most feasible approach is for the securitization facility to be sponsored by domestic government or international donor. Then, subsidy portion of future FiT revenue payments can be securitized at a lower discount rate, resulting in an upfront grant of as high as US$64 million (Table 5) and leverage of the CTF funds of US$1.71 of commercial capital per US$1 of CTF money.

The CTF leverage could be further enhanced by offering a guarantee on the commercial loan with the objective of lowering the cost of borrowing, in this case from 11 percent to 7 percent. This would mobilize about US$2.1 of commercial capital for each US$1 of CTF funding (excluding the cost of the guarantee, see Table 5).

Table 5: Alternative Financial Structure for Wind Energy Project

Parameters	Financing scenarios		
	FiT subsidy paid over useful life	FiT subsidy securitized	FiT subsidy securitized plus loan guarantee
Source of capital			
Sponsors' equity	US$18 million	US$11 million	US$13 million
Commercial debt	US$42 million	US$26 million	US$30 million
Concessional loan	US$100 million	US$59 million	US$52 million
Upfront value of FiT subsidy	US$0 million	US$64 million	US$64 million
Leverage by CTF loan	1 : 0.60	1 : 1.71	1 : 2.10

Source: Authors.

If securitization facility were to be established by private financiers, the size of the upfront grant would only reach US$34 million and would not increase the leveraging factor for CTF money. Moreover, the project would experience difficulties in meeting its debt service obligations, rendering this financial solution to be not viable.

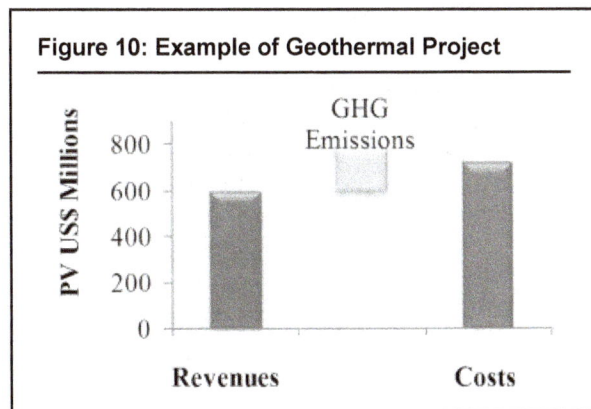

Figure 10: Example of Geothermal Project

Source: Authors.

Green Finance for a Geothermal Project

A 150 MW geothermal project has a capital cost of US$543 million. Adding operation and maintenance costs gives a present value of total costs of US$714 million, while the present value of the project revenue is US$588 million. This leaves a financial viability gap with a present value of US$126 million (Figure 10).

Avoided GHG emissions are valued at US$188 million; benefits from reduced local air pollution total US$45 million.

In this case, the viability gap can be bridged in several different ways. For example, a government can provide subsidies to fully cover local pollution reduction benefits, while the international community can provide the required residual amount against the value of abated global externalities. However, given the scarce resources of many governments of developing countries, it may be more practical for the international community to provide the maximum amount justified on the grounds of the net GHG abatement benefits.

Thus, a concessional loan with an implicit grant of US$126 million could be used as the instrument to close the gap fully. To achieve this level of concessionality, the loan would need to have a 30-year repayment period, a 10-year grace period, and an interest rate of 2.5 percent, as shown in Table 6.

Table 6: Financial Structure for Geothermal Energy Project

Financial Instrument	Amount	Maturity	Grace Period	Cost of Capital	Implicit Subsidy[a]
Concessional Loan	US$138 million	30 years	10 years	2.5%	US$126 million
Commercial Debt	US$240 million	15 years	—	11%	—
Sponsor's Equity	US$165 million	—	—	22%	—
Total	US$543 million				US$126 million

Source: Authors.
a. The implicit subsidy was calculated based on the 14 percent cost of capital and a 30 year timeframe.

The grant equivalent value of the concessional loan equals the US$126 million viability gap. Private finance of US$165 million in equity, and US$240 million in commercial debt, completes the US$543 million project financing. Therefore, US$138 million of concessional finance leverages private finance of US$405 million.

Building Energy Efficiency Project

This final example illustrates another CTF instrument—a risk sharing facility—that could also be used to mobilize private finance (Figure 11).

This energy efficiency example will require an investment of US$2.4 million to reduce the energy consumption of a building by 1,560 MWh over a 15-year period. Given the commercial electricity tariff is 25 cents per kWh, the annual energy savings would amount to US$400,000.

With the cost of capital of the equity financed deal of 20 percent, the present value of the project's revenue from energy savings amounts to US$1.8 million. The viability gap is therefore US$600,000. The developer of the project would prefer to reduce the

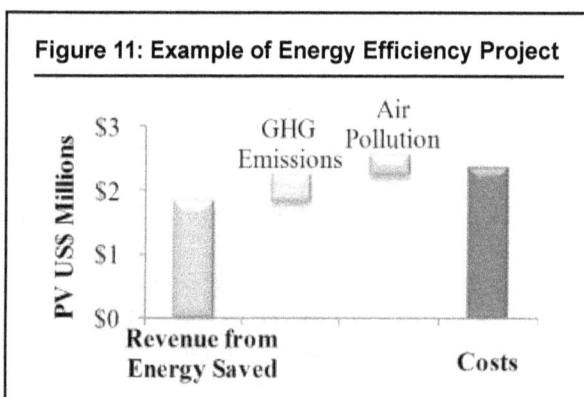

Figure 11: Example of Energy Efficiency Project

Source: Authors.

cost of capital by bringing debt into the project, but prospective commercial lenders perceive the risks to be too high.

The avoided cost of GHG emissions is calculated to be US$400,000—not sufficient to close the viability gap, if it could be monetized. However, the energy efficiency project will avoid local air pollution costs of US$300,000 over the useful life. Therefore, if both the GHG emissions and the air pollution savings could be monetized, then this would be sufficient to close the viability gap. One possible approach is to blend a CTF risk-sharing facility (to cover the GHG emission reduction portion) with an IBRD loan (to cover local pollution reduction portion). Together, these can reduce the cost of capital, thereby making the project profitable.

The present value of the support of US$600,000 needed could be achieved by providing a US$250,000 IBRD loan[E] and a risk-sharing facility to cover 70 percent of the commercial debt in the project. The risk-sharing facility assumes that the project cost of capital would reduce from 20 percent to 12 percent with the introduction of debt. The assumed terms and implicit subsidy of these instruments are provided in Table 7, indicating their grant equivalent values.

The grant equivalent value of the IBRD concessional loan and risk sharing facility equals the US$600,000 viability gap. Along with the US$960,000 in sponsor's equity, the project is able to raise sufficient financing.

Table 7: Financial Structure for Building Energy Efficiency Project

Financial Instrument	Amount	Maturity	Grace Period	Cost of Capital	Implicit Subsidy[a]
Risk Sharing Facility	US$1.20 million	15 years	—	10%	US$0.4 million
IBRD Loan	US$0.25 million	20 years	5 years	5%	US$0.2 million
Sponsor's Equity	US$0.96 million	—	—	20%	—
Total	US$2.41 million				US$0.6 million

Source: Authors.
a. The implicit subsidy was calculated based on the 20 percent cost of capital.

Notes

[A] Lifecycle costs include capital cost, operating cost, maintenance cost, salvage value at the end of ownership or useful life and all other recurring and one-time costs associated with the full life span of the system.

[B] In this example it is assumed that subsidized coal prices are approximately 60 percent of the export price, creating an implicit subsidy to local coal-fired power generation

[C] This is the present value of the additional revenue that the wind plant must earn over its life to provide the higher return that investors demand from a wind farm.

[D] The value of US$34 million reflects present value of additional revenues resulted by the increase of a tariff from the short run marginal cost of a coal-fired plant to the established FiT rate. This is not the present value of total future FiT revenues.

[E] IBRD can only lend to governments, so in practice these funds would have to be lent to government, and then on-lent, possibly through a government-owned financial intermediary, to the project company. For simplicity, we assume that on-lending is on the same terms as the IBRD loan to the government.

CHAPTER 4

Assessment of Green Investment Climate in EAP Countries

The Role of Country Assessment Methodology

Governments can play a pivotal role in promoting investments in climate friendly technologies by adopting a wide range of interventions. Many EAP countries have proposed policies, programs, legislation, institutions, fiscal and financial interventions, and other measures designed to promote green growth of their economies through improving the investment climate.[A] The investment climate for environmentally friendly activities, along with the set of abovementioned measures, is termed here as the "green investment climate."

A country's ability to alter its investment climate differs according to the level of sophistication of its financial markets. A well-developed financial market offers a wide range of instruments through which governments can design their intervention strategies in order to shape their investment climate. While in many cases the effort and the scale of public sector interventions is significant, the measures are often implemented in a piecemeal fashion without an overarching framework.

Research indicates[34] that such a comprehensive framework has not been developed yet. A number of attempts have been made to classify the broad array of possible public interventions and create a coherent approach to how to select the most appropriate ones. Thus, many international organizations, including the United Nations Economic and Social Commission for Asia and Pacific (UNESCAP) Green Growth,[35] Office of Chief Economist of the World Bank,[36] Organisation for Economic Co-operation and Development (OECD),[37] United Nations Environment Programme (UNEP),[38] London School of Economics (LSE),[39] and others, have conducted work in this area. Nevertheless, these attempts have not resulted in a practical, comprehensive, and adaptable to specific country conditions framework that is aimed at promoting green investments.

If such a framework were to be developed, it should be flexible and adaptive to the status and trends of the current investment climate of a given country. Therefore, both an overall evaluation and a detailed assessment of a country's green investment climate must be performed in order to develop a framework capable of bridging in opportunities to create more green investments and thereby reducing the financial viability gap for opportunities that already exist.

The overall evaluation of the green investment climate of countries provides general understanding of attractiveness, prevailing trends, strengths, and other aspects affecting the ability of the country to alter green investment climate. The following section contains an overview of the green investment climate of a number of EAP countries, including China, Indonesia, Malaysia, the Philippines, the Republic of Korea, and Vietnam.

Evaluation of Overall Green Investment Climate in EAP Countries

Annual growth of financial investments in clean energy in 2010 surpassed 30 percent,[40] with China registering the fastest growth rate among the EAP countries as well as at the global level. As a result, China occupies a predominant position among the EAP countries. For instance, the share of gross domestic product (GDP) invested by China in 2009 is five times higher than the United States,[41] reaching US$54.4 billion in 2010 (see Table 8).

Table 8: Key Clean Energy Indicators in EAP Countries

Country	GDP per unit of energy use (2005 PPP$/kg oil eq.)	Energy use per capita (kg oil eq.)	Clean energy investments in 2010[a]	
			(US$ million)	as share of GDP in %
China	3.4	1,484	54,400	1.091
Indonesia	4.1	849	247	0.046
Korea, Rep. of	5.5	4,586	356	0.043
Malaysia	4.7	2,733	n.a.	n.a.
Philippines	7.1	451	200[b]	0.124
Vietnam	3.7	655	200[b]	0.206

Source: Authors' calculations based on data from *The Little Green Data Book,* The World Bank, 2011;[42] *Who's Winning the Clean Energy Race?,* The PEW Charitable Trust, 2011;[43] *Global Trends in Sustainable Energy Investment 2010: Analysis of Trends and Issues in the Financing,* UNEP and Bloomberg, 2010.[44]
a. The figures include only private investments.
b. The figures are rounded and approximate.

Investments in clean energy are driven by energy security, in addition to the global effort to curb climate change and create employment. Measured along these three dimensions, China's 12th Five-Year Plan RE targets are among the world's most ambitious. The Chinese government aims to increase the renewable energy share to 15 percent by 2020, mainly through investments in key sectors such as wind, biomass and solar photovoltaic (PV).[45] To achieve this, China has established FiTs, tax subsidies and other subsidy schemes for wind, rooftop, and building integrated PV along with other renewable energy projects.

During 2008–09, China's National Development and Reform Committee (NDRC) approved a US$218 billion green stimulus package that accounted for almost half of the global expenditures for fiscal interventions.[46] Due to China's commitment to a lower carbon–intensive growth path, the share of coal in China's energy mix is expected to fall to 63 percent from its current level of 70 percent.[47] China's experience offers interesting green development prospects which could be adopted by the other EAP countries with similar characteristics in order to promote their own sustainable growth patterns.

The Chinese experience in promoting energy efficiency utilizing GEF funds summarizes the potentials for leveraging private financing. Table 9 illustrates the scope for leverage using different combinations of financing instruments.

Table 9: Financial Products and Their Use

Financial product	Potential for use	Leverage (IFC: local FI)	Donor role	Donor leverage (donor to FI)
Trade finance	Addresses trade in EE/RE equipment	1:1.3	None/potentially a subsidy	N/A
Long-term credit line	Asset liability matching and liquidity for projects with longer paybacks	1:1.3	Interest or capital subsidy	N/A
Pari-passu risk sharing facilities (funded/unfunded)	Addresses risk perception (soft) and exposure barriers	> 1:2	First loss or subsidy	> 1:5
Subordinated risk sharing facilities (funded or unfunded)	Addresses financing gaps, risk appetite	> 1:3	First loss or subsidy	> 1:15

Source: Adapted from *Scaling up Climate Finance in the Private Sector,* IFC, 2011.[48]

Similarly, the Republic of Korea made solar and wind two key sectors of its green development plan. In 2010, the Korea's total investments in clean energy climbed to US$356 million, almost doubling its total renewable energy capacity from the 2009 level.[49] In 2009–12, the Korea plans to inject US$59.9 billion in its economy as part of its stimulus package. FiTs and tax exemption for dividends are among the incentives provided by the Korean government to foster green energy.[50] While Korea has declared its intention of becoming the world's seventh-largest green power by 2020, the achievement of this goal may be adversely affected by strong overseas energy dependence (see Table 10).

Table 10: Energy Consumption and Imports for the Republic of Korea: 2000–07

Category	Units	2000	2001	2002	2003	2004	2005	2006	2007
Primary Energy Consumption Growth	%	6.4	2.9	5.2	3.1	2.4	3.8	2.1	1.3
Overseas Dependency	%	97.2	97.3	97.1	96.9	96.7	96.6	96.5	96.6

Source: KEMCO, Korea Energy Management Corporation.[51]

Such dependence could negatively influence the country's balance of payments and compromise the achievement of the country's development targets. Therefore, a sound green investment plan is required to mitigate energy dependence-related risks and allow the Korea to achieve its green objectives.

Indonesia and Malaysia have also adopted green stimulus plans, even though the magnitude of their impacts is lower than China and Korea's interventions. In 2010, Indonesia's private investments amounted to US$247 million with geothermal energy the main recipient of such spending. One of Indonesia's key energy targets is the increase of geothermal power through preferential tariffs (such as FiT) and the abolishment of import duties. Ultimately, Indonesia aims to source 15 percent of all electricity from clean energy. Indonesia's energy use per capita is, however, lower than Malaysia (see Table 8), which in turn is high in terms of energy intensity. This is potentially symptomatic of Malaysia's inefficient commitment towards energy conservation measures.

The Philippines lacks strategic policies and has set no specific objectives for GHG reduction. However, the country benefits from an abundance of geothermal energy which suggests that a comprehensive framework to promote green investments should be designed on the specific available resources of a given country.

Vietnam ranks last among the EAP countries considered for this analysis. The data on financial instruments and market-based mechanisms for Vietnam are scarce, but the country's energy balance shows that Vietnam is heavily dependent on oil imports to meet its energy needs. Hence, Vietnam is exposed to high energy risks[52] and can clearly benefit from instituting changes in order to promote more clean energy investments.

Detailed Assessment of Country Green Investment Climate

The overall evaluation of a country's green investment climate should be complemented by a detailed assessment of its four main components: (i) policies and legislation; (ii) financial and economic instruments; (iii) programs and institutions; and (iv) regulatory environment (see Figure 12). Each of these components consists of a number of elements (see the Appendix for a more detailed discussion)

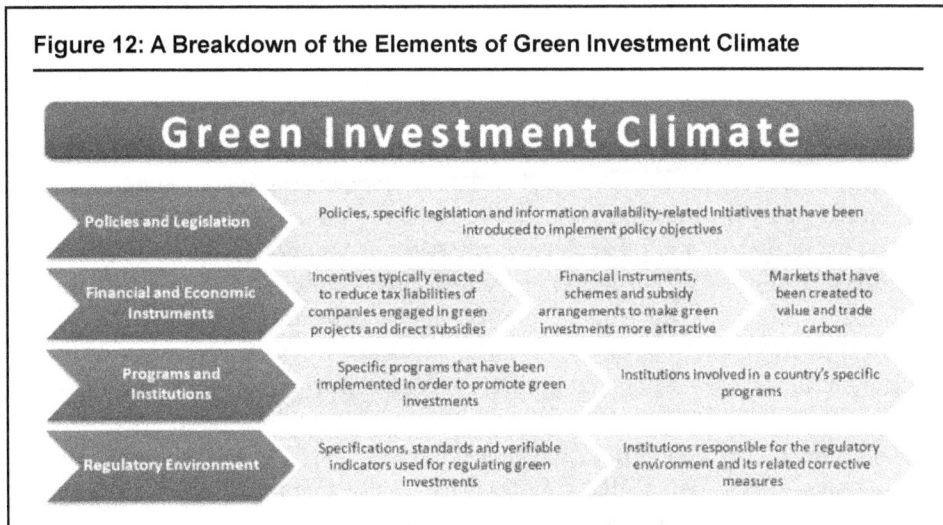

Figure 12: A Breakdown of the Elements of Green Investment Climate

Source: Authors.

- **Policies and legislation** are evaluated as they provide the context to establish financial and economic instruments, along with specific programs and institutions.
- **Financial and economic instruments** are closely examined as they foster the implementation of the abovementioned policies and laws. Such instruments interact with programs and institutions through a variety of channels including market signals, and promote certain activities including investments in research and development.
- **Programs and institutions** often involve different ministries and levels of government, thereby increasing the overall complexity of a country's green investment climate. Such determinants are investigated as they facilitate the adoption of green investments in order to demonstrate viability and reduce excessive perception of risk.

- ▣ **The regulatory environment** is analyzed in order to evaluate the system responsiveness in providing adequate feedback and corrective measures aiding proper functioning of a country's green investment climate.

To provide EAP countries with a point of reference for their green investment climates and to allow them to set realistic expectations for what can be accomplished in the short-, medium- and long-term, the information on the four components of the green investment climate is aggregated and then used to develop a country benchmark.

Benchmarking Green Investment Climate

Countries are adopting pro-green policies at increasing rates and are developing financing schemes and instruments for funding clean investments within their boundaries. Countries with well-developed capital markets and sophisticated tax policies can establish a wide array of both public and private financing options. Governments of these countries are not only focusing on improving the global and domestic environments, but are also recognizing a highly significant opportunity for developing and deploying as well as exporting their green technologies in order to foster industrial growth along with its related income and employment benefits.[B, 53]

For developing countries, the options for national interventions are significantly fewer. Not only do these countries have limited capacity to compete in the area of technology, but their own public funding is constrained by budgetary limitations and competing commitments to other important initiatives such as, health, education, and other basic services, such as water supply and sanitation. Moreover, local capital markets and financial institutions of poorer economies are still not adequately developed, and lack the capacity to develop sophisticated instruments and to mobilize long-term finance.

Consequently, many developing countries rely heavily on donor support through a number of international financing mechanisms such as carbon markets through CDM, the clean investment funds, as well as direct grants. Nonetheless, governments need to contribute to closing the financing gap, especially in policies that distort prices and disadvantage green investments in their own economies.

Therefore, it is essential that countries, especially those with inadequate governance, are guided by a proper benchmark through (i) establishing a monitoring, reporting, and verification (MRV) system, and (ii) utilizing the data to establish an index of green investment finance climate that would be helpful for investors. These steps will allow policy makers to set more realistic goals for the short term as well as to undertake appropriate actions facilitating progress in the medium and long term. Country assessments and benchmarking are needed to determine these expectations as well as to shape the policy dialogue and actions that can reasonably be taken in order to expand the total portfolio of green projects in the medium and longer term.

The results of the benchmarking provide an understanding of the strengths and weaknesses of the green investment climate in any country as well as the ability to assess both the potential and limits for improvements, especially in the short to medium term. These results should also help international donors and funding institutions understand better how and to what extent to deploy their existing instruments and programs.

Notes

[A] The investment climate refers to the economic and market conditions that influence decisions to invest. A sound investment climate provides private firms with opportunities and incentives to invest and is key to sustaining growth. A vibrant private sector creates jobs, provides the necessary goods and services to improve living standards, and contributes taxes to fund health, education, and other public goods. However, all too often potential private sector contributions to development are constrained by unjustified risks, costs, and barriers to competition.

[B] Sorrell and Sijm (2003) note the potential for an "early mover advantage," by which strong, early renewables support could spur the development of viable industries with significant export potential. They find that such a strategy enabled German firms to capture much of the world's wind energy market.

CHAPTER 5

Conclusion and Next Steps

The report has presented a green infrastructure finance framework that can be used to stimulate greater flow of funds for green investments in EAP countries. It is primarily oriented toward promoting private investments, but can also serve to accelerate public-private partnerships as well as purely public engagements.

The framework consists of two complementary components:

1. **Analytical methodology** that will assist policy makers in deriving the financial viability gap of green investments, understanding what comprises the gap, and explaining the causes of this gap in terms of global and local externalities, price distortions and risk premiums;

2. **Country assessment framework** that will allow a better understanding of a country's investment climate in general and green investments climate specifically.

The following benefits can be derived by the implementation of this framework:

- The evaluation and explanation of the gap can determine rapidly whether an investment can be justified on the grounds of climate change (net GHG emission abatement) benefits and to better understand how price distortions in an economy impact the viability of these investments.

- The estimation of what constitutes the viability gap provides a guideline for which portions of the viability gap should be targeted, although the framework does not supply strict prescriptions in this regard.

- Apportioning the viability gap to various stakeholders will determine more accurately the mix of instruments that can be used to close the gap. This can combine international financing mechanisms with government instruments such as feed-in tariff, direct subsidies, and fiscal incentives. The methodology also provides guidance to use these instruments for maximum effect and at least cost to governments.

- The framework will also identify actions that governments can take to improve the various elements of their investment climate and thus increase the scope for financing a greater number of investments with the implementation of those actions.

- The framework provides a sound basis for the identification of those green investments that can already be financed and implemented, given the country's current conditions and ongoing international programs. This approach can further determine the investment projects that are not currently viable but *can be* made viable in the short term through blending financial instruments.

◪ Lastly, nonviable projects that require substantive change in the investment environment can also be identified along with the corresponding set of required policy interventions. Overall, the framework will allow policy makers to evaluate the projects and develop a strategic green infrastructure finance plan.

This process is illustrated in Figure 13, where the intention is to proceed with the piloting of the framework in selected EAP countries.

Figure 13: Process for Pilot Implementation of the Green Infrastructure Finance Framework

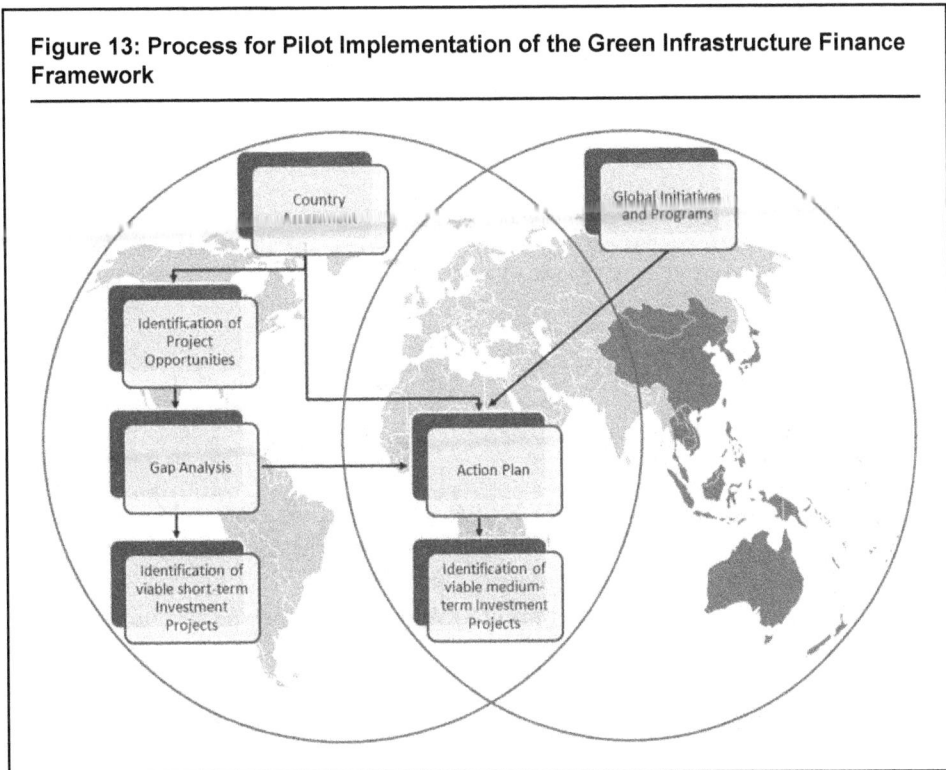

Source: Authors.

Throughout the EAP region and worldwide, the implementation of the Green Infrastructure Finance framework can benefit from further work in the following relevant areas:

◪ **Innovative financing schemes.** This report discusses a number of new schemes, including a viability gap facility, and guarantees or surety to reduce the equity portion of the financing plan. Many innovative schemes that have also been introduced for PPPs, such as hybrid financing schemes, can also be utilized for green investments. While carbon markets improve and ultimately stabilize, there is a need to identify other ways to mobilize international donor support through the identification of innovative solutions and new approaches for financing and implementing green investments. This may mean identifying new ways of blending different financing instruments, international donor support, and approaches to close the financial viability gap or creating more innovative mechanisms in areas that contain the main deficiencies (see Box 6).

Box 6: Mechanism to Subscribe Emission Subsidy Costs

In a highly uncertain environment where the price of carbon is fluctuating widely, an alternative approach in evaluating an "appropriate value" for the externality costs is to obtain the ratio of the capital subsidy required to implement a given clean investment over the quantity of carbon it proposes to reduce. This would provide a benchmark for the relative attractiveness of a given clean project. Clean projects can then be ranked according to the amount of GHG emissions saved per one dollar of subsidy (Emission Subsidy Cost) from the highest cost to the lowest. Then, the subsidies of these projects could be offered for subscription by international donors in a voluntary market through a "market maker" mechanism. Through this mechanism, donors would contribute to closing the funding gap by subscribing to a portion or the entire subsidy required to make the project financially attractive.

Ultimately, the discretion of the donors would determine which projects they would financially support and the criteria used to evaluate the projects may differ between donors. For the projects of a significant size of the financing gap, where a single donor may not be willing to or capable of carrying the entire financing burden and investment risk, a syndication process may be established. Since this scheme proposes to attract upfront financing, the regulatory approach would be based on compliance through the posting of security such as a performance bond. Unlike the CDM system, in-country participating regulatory agencies could be certified to carry out this function and audited by themselves for compliance.

Source: Authors.

- **Benchmarking systems:** A credible benchmarking system would allow governments to assess their own progress in improving their investment climate with an emphasis on low-emission project-related issues.

- **Public-private sector cooperation:** Developing a framework for improved collaboration between public and private sectors could greatly benefit green infrastructure financing mechanisms. This might occur through the development of a practitioners' network that would focus on knowledge exchange and on building working relationships.

- **Technical assistance and coordination between stakeholders from different country:** Coordinated work between stakeholders from different countries will allow policy makers, financial institutions, investors, and developers secure a common understanding of the opportunities and challenges of green infrastructure finance. Accordingly, an experts' panel sponsored by APEC Senior Finance Ministry officials has recommended the establishment of a Green Finance Institute, recognizing that the capacity building requirements are substantial.[54]

- **MRV systems:** As more tradable permit schemes are developed, emerging country governments should consider establishing a cost efficient system of monitoring and verification in order to access the potential financial benefits that these schemes can offer in terms of financial support. For example, the Tokyo Emission Trading Scheme (Tokyo ETS) allows for the issuance of green certificates by projects conducted in other countries. Japanese manufacturers that are seeking opportunities in developing countries can export their technologies at discounts in exchange for sellable verified tradable permits. Such a scheme, which would be highly beneficial to both importer and exporters, can only be achieved under the auspices of a reliable MRV system that generates comparable data across countries. Establishing a credible MRV system will require various models/country case studies of national and sectoral MRV systems. It will also need a thorough analysis of organizational structure, mandates, budgets, human resources, and technical skills. The methodologies currently available for quantifying energy use and CO_2 emissions from various sources covering the supply-side and the end-use sectors will need to be evaluated.

Green Investment Climate Matrix

There are a number of determinants of a country's investment climate. Such determinants also have a strong impact on the risks perceived by private investors and the returns they anticipate from their investments. Several attempts have been made to identify the main determinants of a country's green investment climate and develop a structured approach to assess the efficiency and applicability of public sector interventions in different country and project contexts. This work presents a comprehensive matrix developed by the authors that serves this purpose. Although more research is needed to identify all variables influencing private investments on green-related projects, desk-research has shown that such variables can be grouped into (i) policies and legislation, (ii) financial and economic instruments, (iii) programs and institutions, and (iv) regulatory environment. A graphic breakdown of the subsections of green investment climate is presented in Table 11.

Table 11: Green Investment Climate Matrix

Policies	Financial and economic instruments			Programs and institutions		Regulatory environment	
Policies, targets, and legislation	**Fiscal incentives**	**Financial measures**	**Market-based mechanisms**	**Programs**	**Institutions**	**Procedures and mechanisms**	**Regulatory agencies**
Policies, specific legislation and information availability-related initiatives that have been introduced to implement policy objectives	*Incentives typically enacted to reduce tax liabilities*	*Financial instruments, schemes and subsidy arrangements*	*Markets that have been created to value and trade carbon*	*Specific programs that have been implemented to promote green investments*	*Institutions involved in a country's specific programs*	*Specifications, standards and verifiable indicators for regulating green investments*	*Institutions responsible for the regulatory environment*
• Policies, objectives and targets • Environmental laws • Liability rules • Information availability such as eco-labeling, reporting requirements, energy auditing and best practice guidelines	• Tax credits • Tax deductions • Tax deferrals • Tax-equity swaps • Tax holidays • Loss carry forward • Reduction of levies (income or VAT) • Accelerated depreciation • Subsidies	• Feed-in tariffs • Life-line tariffs • Government loans • Guarantees • Credit lines • Equity funds • Venture capital • Grants • Bonds • Mezzanine	• Cap and trade programs • Baseline and credit programs • Offset schemes • Tradable white certificate schemes • Tradable green certificate schemes	• Voluntary programs • R&D programs • Capacity building programs • Eco-industrial parks • Smart growth zones • Waste exchange • Green Public Procurement • International organizations' programs • Local institutions' programs • Net metering	• Institutions	• Standard specifications • Corrective action plans for ensuring compliance with regulation • Emission monitoring, reporting and verification	• Regulatory agencies ensuring compliance with regulation

Source: Authors.

References

1. IEA (2010), *Energy Technology Perspectives: Scenarios and Strategies to 2050*, Executive Summary, IEA. Retrieved on 03/08/2011 from http://www.iea.org/techno/etp/etp10/English.pdf

2. Wilshire, M. (2009), *Global Futures 2009: Clean Energy Investment not on Track to Prevent Climate Change*, Bloomberg New Energy Finance, March 17, 2009. Retrieved on December 16, 2010 from http://2009.newenergyfinancesummit.com/global%20futures%20executive%20summary.pdf

3. World Bank (2010), *Winds of Change: East Asia's Sustainable Energy Future*, Infrastructure Unit, East Asia and Pacific Region, World Bank. Retrieved on 11/25/2010 from http://siteresources.worldbank.org/INTEASTASIAPACIFIC/Resources/226262-1271320774648/windsofchange_fullreport.pdf

4. UNFCCC (2009), *Report of the Conference of the Parties on Its Fifteenth Session*, Held in Copenhagen from 7 to 19 December 2009, Addendum: Part Two: Action taken by the Conference of the Parties at its fifteenth session, Decision -/CP.15, UNFCCC, Copenhagen, 18 December, 2009. Retrieved on 11/25/2010 from http://unfccc.int/resource/docs/2009/cop15/eng/11a01.pdf

5. UN (2010), *Report of the Secretary-General's High-level Advisory Group on Climate Change Financing*, United Nations, 5 November, 2010. Retrieved on 11/25/2010 from http://www.un.org/wcm/webdav/site/climatechange/shared/Documents/AGF_reports/AGF%20Report.pdf

6. Baietti, A., Shlyakhtenko, A., La Rocca, R., Patel, U. (2011), *Green Infrastructure Finance: Leading Initiatives and Research*, World Bank.

7. Haites, E. (2008), *Investment and Financial Flows Needed to Address Climate Change*, A briefing paper for Breaking the Climate Deadlock, Margaree Consultants, The Climate Group. Retrieved on 11/25/2010 from http://www.theclimategroup.org/_assets/files/Investment-and-Financial-Flows.pdf

8. Ackermann, J. (2010), *Delivering the Next Economy*, Global Metro Summit, Keynote address, Metropolitan Policy Program at Brookings, The Brookings Institute. Retrieved on 12/22/2010 from http://www.brookings.edu/~/media/Files/events/2010/1208_metro_summit/1208_metro_summit_ackermann.pdf

9. Green Investment Bank Commission (2010), *Unlocking investment to deliver Britain's low carbon future*, Report by the Green Investment Bank Commission. Retrieved on 12/22/2010 from http://www.climatechangecapital.com/media/108890/unlocking%20investment%20to%20deliver%20britain's%20low%20carbon%20future%20-%20green%20investment%20bank%20commission%20report%20-%20final%20-%20june%202010.pdf

10. UNIDO (2009), *Investing in and financing Green Business*: Round Table Briefing Note, Global Industry for Global Recovery and Growth, General Conference, Thirteenth

Session, United Nations Industrial Development Organization (UNIDO), 9 December 2009, Vienna International Centre. Retrieved on 12/22/2010 from http://www.unido.org/fileadmin/user_media/UNIDO_Header_Site/Subsites/Green_Industry_Asia_Conference__Maanila_/GC13/Arab_Ebook.pdf

11. Ritchie, D. (2010), *Barriers to Private Sector Investment in the Clean Energy Sector of Developing Countries*, Published by Private Sector Development—Propaco's Magazine in 'Private equity and clean energy: how to boost investments in emerging markets?' Issue 6, May 2010. Retrieved on 11/25/2010 from http://www.proparco.fr/jahia/Jahia/site/proparco/lang/en/pid/70300

12. Taylor, R.P. (2008), *Financing Energy Efficiency: Lessons from Brazil, China, India, and beyond*, World Bank. Retrieved on 01/02/2011 from http://www-wds.worldbank.org/external/default/WDSContentServer/WDSP/IB/2008/02/18/000333037_20080218015226/Rendered/PDF/425290PUB0ISBN11OFFICIAL0USE0ONLY10.pdf

13. McKinsey & Company (2009), *Pathways to a Low Carbon Economy: Version 2 of the Greenhouse Gas Abatement Cost Curve*, McKinsey & Company. Retrieved on December 17, 2010 from http://www.worldwildlife.org/climate/WWFBinaryitem11334.pdf

14. UNFCC (2007), *Investment and Financial Flows to Address Climate Change*, UNFCCC. Retrieved on December 17, 2010 from http://unfccc.int/resource/docs/publications/financial_flows.pdf

15. UNEP (2009), *The Materiality of Climate Change: How Finance Copes with Ticking Clock*. A report by the Asset Management Working Group of the UNEP FI, The third iteration of the AMWG's 'Materiality Series', UNEP, October 2009. Retrieved on 11/25/2010 from http://www.unepfi.org/fileadmin/documents/materiality3.pdf

16. Global Climate Network (2010), *Investing in Clean Energy: How to maximize clean energy deployment from international climate investments*, Global Climate Network discussion paper no. 4, Center for American Progress, November 2010. Retrieved on 12/22/2010 from http://www.americanprogress.org/issues/2010/11/pdf/gcnreport_nov2010.pdf

17. OECD (2010), *Interim Report of the Green Growth Strategy: Implementing Our Commitment for a Sustainable Future*, Meeting of the Council at Ministerial Level, 27-28 May 2010, OECD, 2010. Retrieved on 12/20/2010 from http://www.oecd.org/dataoecd/42/46/45312720.pdf

18. World Economic Forum (2009), *Task Force on Low-Carbon Prosperity: Recommendations*, World Economic Forum. Retrieved on 09/07/2010 from http://www.weforum.org/documents/gov/Environment/TF%20Low%20Carbon%20Prosperity%20Recommendations.pdf

19. Jamison, E., *From Innovation to Infrastructure: Financing First Commercial Clean Energy Projects*, CalCEF Innovation White Paper, June 2010. Retrieved on 11/25/2010 from http://www.calcef.org/innovations/activities/FirstProjFin_0610.pdf

20. IIGCC, *Institutional Investors Group on Climate Change home page: About us*, IIGCC, 2010. Retrieved on 12/22/2010 from http://www.iigcc.org/about-us

21. World Business Council for Sustainable Development, *About Us*, World Business Council for Sustainable Development, 2011. Accessed on 10/30/2011 at http://www.wbcsd.org/about.aspx

22. C40 Cities, *About-Us*, C40 Cities Climate Leadership Group, 2011. Accessed on 10/30/2011 at http://live.c40cities.org/about-us/

23. Carbon War Room, *Strategy and Tactics*, Carbon War Room, 2011. Accessed on 10/30/2011 at http://www.carbonwarroom.com/strategy-and-tactics

24. Stern, N., *The Economics of Climate Change: The Stern Review*. Cambridge: Cambridge University Press, 2007. Retrieved on 02/12/2011 from http://www.cambridge.org/gb/knowledge/isbn/item1164284/?site_locale=en_GB

25. UN Economic Commission for Africa, *Financial Resources and Investment for Climate Change*, UN Economic Commission for Africa, 2009. Retrieved on 11/25/2010 from http://www.oecd.org/dataoecd/29/59/43551000.pdf

26. CIF, *Climate Investment Funds*, Funding Basics, 2008. Accessed on 11/1/2011 at http://www.climateinvestmentfunds.org/cif/funding-basics

27. *Energy Technology Perspectives: Scenarios and Strategies to 2050*, Executive Summary, IEA, 2010. See [1]

28. Price, R and Thornton, S and Nelson, S. (2007), *The Social Cost of Carbon and the Shadow Price of Carbon*, Department for Environment, Food and Rural Affairs, 2007. Retrieved on 10/1/2011 from http://www.decc.gov.uk/assets/decc/what%20we%20do/a%20low%20carbon%20uk/carbon%20valuation/shadow_price/background.pdf

29. *Report of the Secretary-General's High-level Advisory Group on Climate Change Financing*, United Nations, 2010. See [5]

30. GEF, *Global Environment Facility*, What is the GEF, 2010. Accessed on 11/1/2011 at http://www.thegef.org/gef/whatisgef

31. Baker & McKenzie, *Philippines Issues Feed-In Tariff Rules Under Renewable Energy Law*, August 2010. Retrieved on 11/1/2011 from http://www.bakermckenzie.com/ALManilaFeedInTariffRulesAug10/

32. World Resources Institute, Thailand's Approach to Promoting Clean Energy in the Electricity Sector, 2008. Retrieved on 11/1/2011 from http://electricitygovernance.wri.org/files/egi/Thailand.pdf

33. Viboonchart, N., *GE Plans Move into Thai Solar-Energy Market*, The Nation August 8, 2011. Retrieved on 10/01/2011 from http://www.nationmultimedia.com/2011/08/08/business/GE-plans-move-into-Thai-solar-energy-market-30162177.html

34. Baietti, A., Shlyakhtenko, A., La Rocca, R., Patel, U., *Green Infrastructure Finance: Leading Initiatives and Research*, World Bank, 2011. See [6]

35. UNESCAP (2010), *Policies and Instruments: Green Growth Policy Overview*, Green Growth, UNESCAP, 2010. Retrieved on 12/25/2010 from http://www.greengrowth.org/policies.asp

36. World Bank (2010), *Climate Change and Economic Policies in APEC economies: Synthesis Report*, Office of the Chief Economist, East Asia and Pacific Region, World Bank, 2010. Retrieved on 12/10/2010 from http://www-wds.worldbank.org/external/default/WDSContentServer/WDSP/IB/2010/11/30/000333037_20101130235513/Rendered/PDF/565620ESW0WHIT10Report1Nov117102010.pdf

37. de Serres, A., F. Murtin and G. Nicoletti, *A Framework for Assessing Green Growth Policies*, OECD Economics Department Working Papers, No. 774, OECD Publishing, OECD, 2010. Retrieved on 02/20/2011 from http://www.oecd-ilibrary.org/a-framework-for-assessing-green-growth-policies_5kmfj2xvcmkf.pdf;jsessionid=5ojqoli90e5vg.delta?contentType=/ns/WorkingPaper&itemId=/content/workingpaper/5kmfj2xvcmkf-en&containerItemId=/content/workingpaperseries/18151973&accessItemIds=&mimeType=application/pdf

38. Maclean, J., et al, *Public Finance Mechanisms to Mobilise Investment in Climate Change Mitigation*, UNEP SEFI, 2008. Retrieved on 02/20/2011 from http://www.sefi.unep.org/fileadmin/media/sefi/docs/UNEP_Public_Finance_Report.pdf

39. Grantham Institute, *Meeting the Climate Challenge: Using Public Funds to Leverage Private Investment in Developing Countries*, London School of Economics, Grantham Institute, September 2009. Retrieved on 02/21/2011 from http://www2.lse.ac.uk/ GranthamInstitute/publications/Other/Leveragedfunds/Meeting%20the%20Climate%20Challenge.aspx

40. Bloomberg New Energy Finance (2011), *Bloomberg New Energy Finance Summit 2011— Michael Liebreich Keynote*, Bloomberg New Energy Finance, April 2011. Retrieved on 05/07/2011 from http://bnef.com/free-publications/presentations/

41. The PEW Charitable Trust (2010), *"Who's Winning the Clean Energy Race?"*, The PEW Charitable Trust, 2010. Retrieved on 05/07/2011 from http://www.pewtrusts.org/uploadedFiles/wwwpewtrustsorg/Reports/Global_warming/G-20%20Report.pdf

42. World Bank, *The Little Green Data Book*, The World Bank, 2010. Retrieved on 02/25/2011 from http://www.semide.net/media_server/files/semide/topics/water-data/little-green-data-book-2010-world-bank/GreenDataBook2010_WorldBank.pdf

43. *Who's Winning the Clean Energy Race?*, The PEW Charitable Trust, 2011. See [41]

44. UNEP (2010), *Global Trends in Sustainable Energy Investment 2010: Analysis of Trends and Issues in the Financing*, UNEP and Bloomberg, 2010. Retrieved on 11/01/2011 from http://bnef.com/Download/UserFiles_File_WhitePapers/sefi_unep_global_trends_2010.pdf

45. China Greentech Initiative (2011), *China's 12th Five-Year Plan: Implications for Greentech*, China Greentech Initiative, March 2011. Retrieved on 05/07/2011 from http://www.china-greentech.com/sites/default/files/12thFYPImpactonGreentechbyCGTI.pdf

46. Barbier, E.B. (2007), *Linking Green Stimulus, Energy Efficiency and Technological Innovation: The Need for Complementary Policies*, Atlantic Energy Efficiency, 2007. Retrieved on 06/24/2011 from http://igov.berkeley.edu/trans/sites/default/files/Linking%20green%20stimulus%2C%20energy%20efficiency%20and%20technological.ppt

47. *China's 12th Five-Year Plan: Implications for Greentech*, China Greentech Initiative (2011). See [45]

48. Narayanan, A., *Scaling up Climate Finance in the Private Sector: Leveraging Public Funding to Catalyze the Private Sector*, IFC, 2011. Retrieved on 10/01/2011 from http://europa.eu/epc/pdf/workshop/4-6_ajay_narayanan_presentation_-__brussels_april_12_2011_en.pdf

49. *Who's Winning The Clean Energy Race?*, The Pew Charitable Trusts, 2010. See [41]

50. European Union, *Assessing the Implementation and Impact of Green Elements of Member States' National Recovery Plans*, 2011. Retrieved on 11/01/2011 from http://ec.europa.eu/environment/enveco/memberstate_policy/pdf/green_recovery_plans.pdf

51. Korea Energy Management Corporation (2011), Energy Review In Korea, Korea Energy Management Corporation, 2011. Accessed on 06/24/2011 from http://www.kemco.or.kr/new_eng/pg02/pg02040400.asp

52. IEA (2011), *Vietnam Energy Balance in 2008*, IEA, 2011. Accessed on 05/07/2011 at http://www.iea.org/stats/balancetable.asp?COUNTRY_CODE=VN

53. Sorrell, S. and J. Sijm, (2003), *Carbon trading in the policy mix*, Oxford Review of Economic Policy, 19(3), 420-437, 2003. Retrieved on 10/01/2011 from http://oxrep.oxfordjournals.org/content/19/3/420.short

54. APEC, *Green Finance for Green Growth*, 17th Finance Ministers' Meeting Kyoto, 2010/FMM/006 Agenda Item: Plenary 2, Japan, 5-6 November 2010. Retrieved on 10/20/2011 from http://aimp.apec.org/Documents/2010/MM/FMM/10_fmm_006.pdf

ECO-AUDIT
Environmental Benefits Statement

The World Bank is committed to preserving endangered forests and natural resources. The Office of the Publisher has chosen to print World Bank Studies and Working Papers on recycled paper with 30 percent postconsumer fiber in accordance with the recommended standards for paper usage set by the Green Press Initiative, a non-profit program supporting publishers in using fiber that is not sourced from endangered forests. For more information, visit www.greenpressinitiative.org.

In 2010, the printing of this book on recycled paper saved the following:

- 11 trees*
- 3 million Btu of total energy
- 1,045 lb. of net greenhouse gases
- 5,035 gal. of waste water
- 306 lb. of solid waste

---

* 40 feet in height and 6–8 inches in diameter

green
press
INITIATIVE

www.ingramcontent.com/pod-product-compliance
Lightning Source LLC
Chambersburg PA
CBHW051232200326
41519CB00025B/7340